Discrimination

Concepts in the Social Sciences

Series Editor: Frank Parkin

Published Titles

Concepts in the Social Sciences

Discrimination

Michael Banton

Open University Press
Buckingham · Philadelphia

Open University Press
Celtic Court
22 Ballmoor
Buckingham
MK18 1XW

and

1900 Frost Road, Suite 101
Bristol, PA 19007, USA

First Published 1994
Reprinted 1997

A catalogue record of this book is available from the British Library

ISBN 0-335-19191-6 (pbk)   0-335–19192-4 (hbk)

Library of Congress Cataloging-in-Publication Data

Banton, Michael P.
     Discrimination/by Michael P. Banton.
          p.   cm.   (Concepts in the social sciences)
     Includes bibliographical references and index.
     ISBN 0-335-19192-4 (hb.)   ISBN 0-335-19191-6 (pbk.)
     1. Discrimination. 2. Discrimination – Law and legislation.
   I. Title. II. Series.
   JC575.B37   1994
305–dc20   93-32028
                                                                                CIP

Typeset by Type Study, Scarborough
Printed in Great Britain by St Edmundsbury Press,
Bury St Edmunds, Suffolk

Contents

Acknowledgements

At an early stage of my work on this topic I was greatly helped by advice from Professor Donald Horowitz of the Duke University Law School. Since then I have benefited from the advice of Dr Malcolm Evans who lectures on international law at the University of Bristol and Dr John Goering of the United States Department of Housing and Urban Development. I thank them and my students who over the years have taught me to express my arguments as simply as possible!

List of Abbreviations

ACAS	Advisory, Conciliation and Arbitration Service
BCS	British Crime Survey
CEDAW	Convention on the Elimination of Discrimination against Women
CRE	Commission for Racial Equality
EC	European Commission
ECHR	European Convention on Human Rights
EEOC	Equal Employment Opportunity Commission
EOC	Equal Opportunities Commission
EU	European Union
ICCPR	International Covenant on Civil and Political Rights
ICERD	International Convention on the Elimination of Racial Discrimination
ICESCR	International Covenant on Economic, Social and Cultural Rights
ILO	International Labour Office
UCCA	Universities Central Council for Admissions
UDHR	Universal Declaration of Human Rights
UN	United Nations

1
Introduction

In almost all the religions of the world the positions of leadership are held by men. Most adherents of these religions do not think of this as discrimination against women, because discrimination is thought to be bad. Yet minorities within most of them assert that there are no good religious reasons for such practices, and that they *are* discriminatory. Whether or not the minorities are right depends upon the definition of discrimination.

Confusion arises when the parties to such a dispute rely upon a definition which combines the objective component, i.e., the reservation of positions to men, with the moral judgement that such a reservation is, or is not, justified. Further confusion results if discrimination is defined at the outset as being both bad and unlawful. It is possible to get caught in lengthy arguments about whether some practice is discriminatory whenever the disputants start from the associations of the word discrimination in their everyday lives. The only way through this sort of tangle is to employ a purely objective definition of discrimination, as the differential treatment of persons supposed to belong to a particular class of persons (which means that the differential access of men and women to positions of religious leadership *is* discriminatory) and then go on to consider whether or not the difference is morally justified or lawful. There are many circumstances in which reasonable people will disagree about moral justification, while the law relating to discrimination is constantly changing.

It is not possible to determine that an action is discriminatory without indicating the basis of the differential treatment. Discrimination on grounds of sex (or gender) occurs when someone supposed to be female is treated differently from someone supposed to be male (or vice versa). The United Nations Charter (1945) declares in article 55 that the United Nations will promote human rights and fundamental freedoms for all 'without distinction as to race, sex, language or religion'. To these four grounds of possible discrimination another eight were added three years later in the Universal Declaration of Human Rights (UDHR). These were colour, political or other opinion, national or social origin, property, birth or other status, and, since these were given only as examples, there was an implication that the list could be extended.

For legal purposes, whether or not a particular ground is listed may be crucial, but social analysis should look wider and embrace all kinds of differential treatment. For example, in many places people over a certain age, 'senior citizens', are allowed cheaper rates when travelling on public transport or using public facilities, like cinemas and swimming pools. Many institutions have 'supporters' clubs' of some kind and confer privileges on members. The publishers of academic journals often have different subscription rates for individuals as opposed to institutions. Societies like the American Sociological Association and the British Sociological Association have differential subscription rates for people in different income categories, while employers who provide parking facilities for their employees may charge differential rates according to their income. All these are examples of lawful discrimination, but, of course, their justifiability is always open to challenge.

Some commentators try to distinguish discrimination from differentiation. They cite examples of circumstances in which they think it morally justifiable to draw a distinction based on race or sex and call these differentiation as opposed to discrimination. But it is too easy to argue by way of examples chosen to suit the speaker's own argument. Definitions must be able to deal with borderline cases and circumstances in which moral judgements conflict. Later chapters go on to discuss many such cases and circumstances, based upon problems that have come before the courts.

The morality of discrimination is less easily decided than the legality of discrimination. The Catholic Church refers to scriptural authority and church tradition for its conception of the priesthood (and until recently disabled men needed a dispensation before they could be ordained priests). There are very few women in positions of religious leadership in Judaism and Islam either, and some adherents of all three religions would consider it positively immoral for women to occupy such positions. In Saudia Arabia women may not drive motor cars, and when as a protest a number of them did so, it was the religious police who intervened. The morality of discrimination is often the more contentious because it necessarily concerns a class of persons, overlooking the differences between individual members of the class. Dispute may also turn on the magnitude of the difference. Not all 'senior citizens' have a lower income than younger people. It may be thought justified to charge them or the low-paid 20 per cent less for some service, but not to charge them 80 per cent less. Once the discussion leaves the realm of facts and enters that of judgement, it is necessary to look at each case on its merits while trying to be consistent with decisions reached earlier in cases of a similar nature.

/So defined, discrimination is a general feature of social life./The family, the ethnic group and the state are all based on discrimination./Family life is the outcome of beliefs that husband and wife, parent and child, kin, and relatives in varying degrees all have obligations requiring particular kinds of behaviour.)Ethnic groups exist where people identify with others of similar ancestry; the act of identification results in feelings of belonging together and therefore of responsibility towards fellow members of the group. States confer the rights of citizenship upon some individuals and not upon others. There are many criticisms of the lack of correspondence between the realities of family life and the ideal image; fellow feeling can become ethnic chauvinism, while the states of 'Fortress Europe' are reproved for their reluctance to recognize the human rights of asylum-seekers. Yet these are criticisms of practice and do not deny that rights and obligations can be associated only with classes of persons. That association means that members of such classes are treated differently from non-members.

Discrimination occurred in the middle of the nineteenth century as it does now, although there was then no concept of discrimination. Nowhere were women allowed to vote, and this distinction between men and women went almost unchallenged. The democratic principle of the equality of citizens was gaining adherents, but throughout Europe distinctions of social rank between aristocrats of varying degree, gentlefolk and ordinary people, were taken for granted. In the United States some whites believed that blacks, whites, yellows and 'Indians' were separate species so that the relations between people of different race could never be the same as the relations between people of the same race. The prevailing pattern of racial distinction was regarded as the outcome of natural difference, not as the cumulative effect of decisions taken by men and women. Within the caste system of India, and in other parts of the non-white world, differences associated with ancestry, appearance and ethnicity were unquestioned. Differences of custom were thought to reflect differences in essential identity. A fourth-century Chinese chronicler explained 'If he is not of our race, he is sure to have a different mind' (Dikötter 1992: 3).

The social sciences have developed since the mid-nineteenth century. One of their greatest achievements has been to explain why those of different race are of different mind. Earlier it was only the unusual intellect that questioned the view of the world accepted by the rest of society. The social scientist now says that those brought up in a particular culture share a consciousness of the world. The nature of that consciousness is influenced by the environment, the people's history and their institutions – including their religion, their scientific knowledge and the media of communication. As the educated public now knows, it is such factors that cause peoples to be 'of different mind'. The great growth in knowledge about the nature of human society has helped ordinary people to make comparisons that could not have occurred to their great-grandparents; as a result they take less for granted and are more ready to identify forms of discrimination.

The Chinese writer's reference to race was probably a reference to people of the same ancestry. This older sense of the word was swamped in the nineteenth century by the theory that human races – three, five, eight, or more in number – were permanent types, separately created. Though the discoveries of Charles Darwin and the advances of modern genetics have shown this theory to be quite false, its effects have lingered and caused much confusion. Some people think that the very idea of racial discrimination presupposes a concept of race, and since by that they mean the old discredited notion of type, they fear that laws against racial discrimination serve to keep alive out-dated beliefs.

Laws against discrimination may permit a transport company to operate lower charges for senior citizens or to have separate waiting rooms for women passengers. These laws regulate the public sphere only; they do not seek to influence the choice of friends or marriage partners; they do not, in Britain, make illegal a bequest in the will of someone who wants to support a charity for people of ethnic origin similar to himself or herself. This means that unlawful discrimination is a sub-class of the larger class of discriminatory actions. The point needs to be established because social scientists study all forms of discrimination. Whereas in law discrimination is discontinuous (an action is either discriminatory or not), in social science it is a variable. The incidence of discrimination varies both in frequency and in the magnitude of the differential treatment.

Often there is only indirect evidence of the treatment in question. As Chapter 3 will illustrate, it is possible to collect information on all the persons applying for student places in a particular university, their race, gender, age, disability, educational qualifications, the balance of demand relative to supply of places on particular courses, etc. If, after allowing for all relevant factors, a smaller proportion of places has been allocated to applicants of one race or gender, this indicates that discrimination has occurred. Further analysis may reveal the stages in the process primarily responsible for the difference. The individuals responsible might be quite unaware that they were applying discriminatory criteria to the cases with which they had to deal.

Not all applicants for university entrance start equal. Some have had the advantage of more expensive schooling than others. Relative advantage and disadvantage spring from many causes. For example, if parents choose to speak within the home in a language other than that used in the classroom, it is possible that their children may be at a disadvantage compared with their classmates, but no one has discriminated against them. As explained in Chapters 2 and 3, discrimination is one possible cause of inequality or disadvantage; only if other possibilities have been eliminated may it be identified as the prime cause. When discussing causes, it is helpful to follow the practice in philosophy of distinguishing between the *explanandum* (that which is to be explained) and the *explanans* (that which explains). Disadvantage is in this setting the *explanandum*; discrimination is the *explanans*, a postulated cause of the inequality of treatment; though when someone goes on to consider *why* it is that some classes of people discriminate, then discrimination becomes the *explanandum*. As few things cause more confusion in argument than failure to be clear about what it is that has to be explained, and what is being examined as a possible explanation of it, these two Latin words are helpful in observing that distinction (their plural forms are *explananda* and *explanantia*).

Discrimination is an individual action, but, since, by definition, members of the same class are treated similarly, it is simultaneously a social pattern of aggregate behaviour. Since it is social, discrimination at one point in time has consequences for behaviour on subsequent occasions. Patterns of inequality established in one generation are easily transmitted to subsequent generations because people grow up regarding them as right and natural.)

For an action to be discriminatory in law, there must first be a law, and this must define the prohibited grounds of action, the persons protected by the law, and the circumstances in which they are protected. The lawyer's concept of the ground, or cause, of an action is not quite the same as the philosopher's concept of an intention or purpose: people are conscious of their intentions and purposes, whereas their actions can spring from grounds of which they are unaware or are unwilling to acknowledge. A ground is more like a motive. A whole series of actions by the same person can be motivated by ambition, or jealousy, or greed, but there will be some variation in intention from one action to another. If the action is successful, it may be one step in the course of fulfilling an ambition or satisfying a feeling of jealousy. Motives are often mixed, and people may be unaware of some of the forces that stimulate their behaviour. The grounds of an action are therefore something more than the reasons the person himself or herself would offer as an explanation. They are the factors which an independent observer or tribunal identifies as the causes or reasons for an action. It may be easier to grasp the significance of this after a very brief and more general review of the history of legislation against discrimination, and after reference to the tests applied in British and United States courts when it is necessary to determine whether or not discrimination has been present in particular cases.

The first recorded use of the word 'discrimination', in the sense with which this book is concerned, was in a speech by the US President Andrew Johnson in 1866 when he vetoed a civil rights bill. He observed that 'Congress can repeal all state laws discriminating between whites and blacks in the subjects covered by this bill.' That bill was enacted despite his veto. The Congress of the United States declared that African Americans were citizens like other Americans and should enjoy the same rights deriving from that citizenship. This conception of citizenship has been the source of action against discrimination in the United States, but the concept of discrimination did not enter the ordinary English language until later. Its intellectual career started in the late 1940s in the United States when sociologists like R.M. MacIver (1948) taught the post-war generation to distinguish between discrimination as a form of behaviour and prejudice as an attitude. Either one could lead to the other, but a prejudiced person did not necessarily or always discriminate and discrimination was not necessarily the result of prejudice.

At this time discrimination was discussed only with reference to race. It is probable that the first occasion on which it was used in a legal instrument in a more general sense was in 1958, when the Discrimination (Employment and Occupation) Convention of the International Labour Office (ILO) defined discrimination as 'any distinction, exclusion or preference made on the basis of race, colour, sex, religion, political opinion, national extraction or social origin. . .' etc. This may also have been the first important legal instrument to employ the expression 'equality of opportunity' as something to be promoted.

Many other countries find it easier to amend their constitutions than does the United States, and by constitutional amendment or statute law they have progressively extended their law's protections against discrimination to cover more and more classes of persons. In some countries' national debates it is argued that the protected classes should be further extended to include those of age, disability, sexual orientation, accent, and other grounds of discrimination.

Laws against discrimination do not prevent an employer from dismissing an inefficient worker because he or she is of a particular race or sex. They prohibit an employer from dismissing a worker *on the grounds* of that worker's race or sex. For this purpose it is irrelevant whether the worker is of the race or sex the employer believes. What is in question is why the employer tried to dismiss the employee. In most of the countries that have laws against discrimination an employer is not permitted to dismiss a worker because he or she is Jewish. Whether the worker is or is not Jewish does not matter so long as the employer believes the worker to be Jewish, and even if the employer denies that he believed this, it is still open to a tribunal to decide that this was in fact the ground of the employer's action. The law does not depend upon any scientific concept of race. It is similar with sex: though laws are written in terms of sex as a biological class, they are concerned in practice with gender as a social class. A tribunal can sanction an employer for dismissing a person on the grounds of sex without any medical examination to determine whether the person's biological sex corresponded to that person's presentation of himself or herself as male or female. What the law does is to say that employers may not act on the basis of certain grounds.

Just as the law defines certain protected classes, so it defines protected fields. A person may invite to a party only members of a particular race or persons of a particular gender; that is a private decision. The law attempts to prohibit discrimination in *public* life, and the statutes have to specify in which fields of that life their sanctions will operate. In Great Britain and the United States the main protected fields are those of the administration of justice, employment, education, housing, and the provision of goods, facilities and services. They are defined carefully, so that in the US they permit 'affirmative action' on behalf of minorities. In Britain they permit 'positive action' (which does not involve quotas) and they recognize that in certain circumstances being of a particular ethnic origin may be a genuine occupational qualification.

Legislation against discrimination has advanced greatly since the big thrust of the 1960s (1964 in the US, 1965 in Britain). It presents a paradoxical picture in that while the conceptual apparatus of definitions is extremely complex, once the facts have been sorted out and the parties have decided just what the issue is that has to be determined, then matters are often quite simple. Part of the difficulty is that those who live in modern industrial societies play many roles and belong in many classes of persons. If they complain of unfair treatment, the issue then becomes that of deciding if they were treated unfavourably on an unlawful ground. Sometimes it may not be possible to answer this question without knowing more about what has happened to other people belonging in the same class. The effect of discrimination may be to create or increase inequalities between classes of persons, but the existence of such inequalities may also make discrimination more frequent.

The individual and social features of discrimination are combined in its definition as an individual action affecting a particular person who is treated differently because he or she is thought to belong in a particular class of persons. In seeking criteria as to whether an action is, or is not, discriminatory, it is best first to take guidance from the law, while remembering that discriminatory acts do not occur in isolation; they are parts of patterns of behaviour towards women, blacks, disabled people, etc., and they vary greatly from one culture to another. Evidence about discrimination within a particular society is often quantitative, indicating the probability that someone will experience discrimination or the degree of discrimination (because in market situations discrimination may result in someone's being charged more, or having to reach a higher standard, rather than resulting in simple rejection). To analyse these aspects it is necessary to turn to the social sciences. Economists have formulated theories to explain the differences in male and female earnings, the different percentages of women and blacks in given occupations, and so on. Psychology can illuminate why it is that some individuals are more inclined to discriminate than others. Sociologists tackle such questions as why discrimination occurs in particular relationships, why it is only certain kinds of people who are conscious of unequal treatment are willing to pursue grievances, why doctrines promoting discrimination are disseminated, and how discriminatory practices come to characterize particular kinds of social structure, such as the apartheid system in South Africa.

It should now be clear that discrimination is a concept of increasing importance both in the social sciences and in the world of action to protect human rights. It is also a concept that is still in the course of development. Its implications have not been fully worked out and even its basic character is not always understood. Its development is being driven by the very practical concerns of those who want better justice, but these very concerns have sometimes raised obstacles to clear thinking. People who saw apartheid as the prime manifestation of racial discrimination (a paradigm case, as philosophers might say) often concentrated upon what was specific to South Africa and neglected the generality of discrimination. When someone, examining a set of figures, has claimed that they revealed a pattern of discrimination this has not been regarded as a morally-neutral statement, but as an accusation which has provoked a defensiveness likely to interfere with any examination of the facts. An introductory book must therefore show how this concept can be used in the analysis of quantitative information about social patterns and help inform those who wish to measure or reduce the incidence of unjustified discrimination. It has to explain what logically follows from the adoption of a particular definition, admitting the possibility that sometimes the law diverges from logic.

2
Supply and Demand

Everywhere, it seems, the proportion of females studying engineering is much smaller than the proportion studying arts subjects. In Europe and North America black people are often over-represented relative to white people as entertainers, athletes and sporting figures. In these fields a person's individual abilities can be demonstrated for everyone to see, so that the incidence of discrimination is lower, and members of minorities are therefore attracted to them. This helps explain some of the inequalities in the representation of people in certain fields of activity, but not the smaller number of female engineers. Where women and ethnic minority members are more evenly represented there may still be differences in rank and income. Figures of average earnings for many occupations show women to be earning substantially less than men. Such inequalities exist in the present, but they also continue over time, being transmitted from one generation to the next.

If, in a particular occupation, the proportion of women or blacks is smaller than their proportion in the pool from which people seek entry to that occupation, this indicates that women or blacks are at a disadvantage in the recruitment process. Any form of handicap associated with membership in a particular class of persons constitutes disadvantage. A figure showing a class of persons to be under-represented is not by itself evidence of disadvantage because members of a privileged class will not seek entry to a low status occupation, so their under-representation in it would not derive from a handicap. Disadvantage is a feature of selection. It can come about when members of one class of persons are less inclined to put themselves forward as candidates for selection, or when they are less well qualified than others. These are characteristics of the supply of labour. Disadvantage can also come about because employers, faced with equally-qualified candidates, choose fewer proportionately from one class. This is discrimination, and it characterizes the demand for labour.

Differences in labour supply

There are three main general factors which may make the services of female workers or people from the minority ethnic groups less valuable to employers. The first is experience. A woman who interrupts her career to bring up children may, when she returns to the labour market, be at a disadvantage compared to others who have kept abreast of new developments in her occupation. Immigrant workers may have less experience than native workers in the use of equipment and less knowledge of how to set about tasks. Since immigrant workers are often of a distinctive ethnicity, there may be an association between ethnic minority status and the lack of relevant work experience.

A second factor which can lead to differences in the value of labour is motivation. Because of the way they have been brought up or because of their aspirations as individuals, women not may be as concerned as their masculine equivalents to pursue a career. Some of them may regard home-making and the bringing up of children as offering more opportunity for self-fulfilment or as being more important to them in one phase of their life-cycle. They may, therefore, be less highly motivated to seek maximum earnings from wage employment. Anticipation of different career paths may help account for differences apparent among teenagers in school. In 1986–87 in Britain at around the age of 15, equal numbers of males and females attempted examinations in Mathematics, and similarly, equal numbers attempted English. Two years later twice as many males as females attempted Mathematics, while twice as many females as males took the examination paper in English. The pupil peer group had apparently come to regard the one as a male subject and the other as a female subject. It is in such ways that the basis is laid for a segregated job market. School inspectors have concluded that girls are more likely to develop high aspirations in single-sex schools, and it is these schools which seem best able to prevent the stereotyping of subjects as appropriate to pupils of one sex. Peer group pressures do much to maintain different expectations of male and female roles.

Variations in motivation have also been discerned in the labour supply of immigrant minorities. A distinction has been drawn between refugees and economic migrants. Refugees hope to return to the country they have had to leave. They may, therefore, be less disposed to adapt to social expectations in the country in which they have found refuge. They are likely to be less career-oriented and their earnings have been shown to be on average lower than those of economic migrants, who respond strongly to financial incentives. Studies show that in the United States the earnings of economic migrants catch up with those of native workers after 11 to 16 years and thereafter they earn more. Their stronger motivation is transmitted to their children, whose earnings are also higher than the average.

While motivation can be a factor contributing to inequalities in employment and earning, it should be noted that labour supply can be affected by labour demand or perceptions of demand. Women and ethnic minority workers may believe – sometimes justifiably – that, because of the prejudices of employers or their existing employees, they have little chance of securing certain kinds of job. If they believe it not worth their training for such jobs, they will rarely apply for them. This has been called the 'chill factor'. Motivation can also affect readiness to join trade unions and thereby to exert bargaining power.

A further general factor bearing upon labour supply is that of investment. Parents may pay more for the education of their male than their female children. Ethnic minority groups may differ in their attitudes towards children. In some groups parents like to have many children, perhaps because of expectations in the country from which they have come. In others, parents prefer to have fewer children and to spend more on their upbringing. In the United States, Barry Chiswick (1988) has compared the earnings of various minorities, foreign-born and native: European, black, Mexican, Japanese, Chinese, Filipino, and American Indian. He found earnings to be associated with investment in the form of schooling, family size and parental attention. Up to their teens children benefit from having a parent who gives them time. Once they become teenagers they benefit less from parents' time and more from their parents' earning power. Chiswick's research suggests that children's subsequent earnings are higher if there is a parent at home during the early years and if that parent later goes back to paid employment. The 'investment' factors therefore cover not just money spent on schooling but everything conducive to emotional stability and help in the process of growing up.

Experience, motivation and investment are general factors, but there are also factors affecting relative success in particular occupations. Women are less likely to succeed in a job like labouring or furniture-moving which demands physical strength. Men may be less successful as midwives if women prefer to be attended by other women when in childbirth. In those societies in which females are brought up to be less aggressive than males, women may often be better than men in positions which require interpersonal skills.

Differences in the demand for labour

There are three main reasons why employers may have lesser demand for the services of women or ethnic minority workers, even in circumstances in which an objective analysis might show that their services were as valuable as those of male workers belonging to the ethnic majority. If the services of workers in the two categories are equally valuable, any difference in the demand is evidence of discrimination. So sex discrimination and racial discrimination in employment are characteristics of demand. The chief sources are those of taste, risk and profit.

'Taste' may seem a strange word to use in this connection. It is customary to speak of consumers exercising a taste or a preference when they buy one sort of product rather than another, whether the product be a foodstuff, a brand of petrol or an item of clothing. The expression of a prejudice is surely quite different? In some respects it is indeed different, but there are important similarities in market relations. A white woman who wants to sell her house might not wish to sell to a black purchaser, either because of her own feelings or because of what she believes to be the feelings of her neighbours. But if a black purchaser offers a much higher price than any white purchaser is willing to pay, there must come a point at which she will sell to that purchaser. If whites would pay, say, £100 000 and the black purchaser has to bid up to £110 000 in order to buy, the difference of £10 000 represents the price which the seller puts upon her prejudice or taste for selling to someone of her own colour. (For the purchaser, £10 000 represents the 'colour tax'.)

Although the influence of taste is most obvious in consumer purchasing, the concept of taste itself can be applied in a wide range of situations. White male workers, either executives or workers on the factory floor, often form a group of comrades who meet and socialize during breaks or after work. They use language of a kind that is not supposed to be used with women present and may tell jokes they would not expect men from ethnic minorities to appreciate. These are cosy arrangements they wish to preserve. So managers have resisted the appointment of women executives and they have discriminated against job applicants from the ethnic minorities in the belief that they would not be acceptable to the existing labour force. But they may resist only up to the point at which it becomes too expensive to go on discriminating. This reveals the price they put upon their taste for continuing in their accustomed ways.

A second cause of discrimination arises from the lack of the information necessary to calculate the degree of risk. Let us say that an employer has to engage a large number of young workers. Since more women will become mothers and then seek maternity leave or give up their jobs, employers may believe that the female labour turnover will be higher than the male turnover and occasion higher costs in recruiting and training replacements. They will know that not all young women will leave, but may believe simply that, on average, more will do so (and they could be right). Detailed examination of each applicant to try to discover who is likely to stay might be too expensive to be worthwhile. If such an employer decided to engage only males none would ever discover whether the employer's estimate of relative risk was accurate or not. A similar process can affect the recruitment of ethnic minority workers when employers believe that, on average, they are less suitable for some kind of job and when it costs too much to collect sufficient information about individuals to identify the ones who depart from the average. Since the discrimination results from estimates about groups, this has been called the statistical theory of racism and sexism (Phelps 1972), but it is not limited to racial and sex groups. Employers may be unwilling to engage disabled people, for example, because they overestimate the risks involved. Police officers may believe that a disproportionate number of persons arrested for the unlawful possession of drugs are young blacks or young males with long hair. They could then conclude that they were more likely to uncover such offences if they were to stop and search such young men even if they had no grounds for suspecting the particular individuals. This would also be a form of discrimination resulting from a belief about probabilities.

Can anyone profit from discrimination? If women or people from the ethnic minorities can do the work as well as white men, there can be no profit to the employer in excluding them. Under conditions of perfect competition, with every section of the labour force working to the limit of its abilities, the national income would be maximized. There would be more to share out. Some white males might do less well, but most of them would be sharing households with women whose earnings would be higher because there was no discrimination; the benefits would be to some extent shared. Possibilities of profit from situations of imperfect competition arise when a businessman or woman is in a position either of monopoly (he or she is the only seller and there are many buyers) or monopsony (he or she is the only buyer and there are many sellers). Thus, employers in the South African mining industry, seeking black labour, in 1912 established a Native Recruiting Corporation to recruit workers at standard rates. This was a monopsony which maximized their bargaining power in dealing with unorganized workers. Because of it they were able to pay their workers less than they would have done had they bid against one another. South Africa has offered an example of a triangular relationship between the (white) employer, the higher-paid (white) section of the labour force, and the lower-paid (black) section which was forbidden until recently to form trade unions. Because the higher-paid section had greater bargaining power, it could get for itself a bigger share of the employer's wage bill and therefore profit from its power position. In such a situation the employer may be no better off; it will then be advantageous to redefine jobs so that they can be given to black workers who cost less. Any measure that excludes competition from a new source of labour is likely to benefit existing employees but is unlikely to benefit employers. They can profit not from discriminating against the employment of such workers, but from employing them at lower rates than existing workers. They can do this the more easily if women and minority workers are less committed to trade unionism, or are prevented from joining unions.

Transmitted inequality

Advantage and disadvantage are both transmitted from one generation to the next. It is said that in capitalist society the system operates to ensure that working-class children are brought up to do working-class jobs. This is not an argument to pursue now, but it is mentioned here for an important reason. If there are figures showing that women or blacks are at a disadvantage, this may be due to gender or race, but it may also be due in some part to social class if the groups being compared are not of similar class composition.

Advantage and disadvantage are also transmitted by the factor of investment already mentioned. Research suggests that there is less emotional and financial investment in the upbringing of children when the child's parents separate, and particularly if the child is brought up with a step-parent. The effect is more marked than when one parent dies and the child is brought up by the surviving parent. Research in Britain has calculated that if the likelihood of a child brought up by both parents leaving home because of friction is put at 1.0, the likelihood of the child leaving if brought up with a lone mother is 1.4, while if with a step-family it is 3.45, nearly three-and-a-half times as great as the first figure. Children of divorced parents are more likely to leave school early, to cohabit, marry or become a parent before the age of 20. They are more likely to become delinquents and more likely to be unemployed in their thirties.

The children of some divorced parents may grow up in more favourable circumstances than some children in homes with both parents, but the figures show that to grow up in a step-family is to grow up with a significant handicap. Some children overcome this handicap, but allowance should be made for its possible effect when comparisons are made, because the rates of parental separation are higher in some social classes and ethnic groups than in others. The desirability of allowing for family background factors as contributory to disadvantage is a further argument for the advisability of analysing such influences objectively before attempting to draw moral conclusions from the figures.

Competition

When there is a plentiful supply of labour relative to the demand for it, an employer can more easily discriminate on grounds of gender, race or disability. Women, members of ethnic minorities and the disabled have made their greatest advances in the job market in times of war, when the native males have been away and employers have had to compete for labour, bringing on to the market women who might otherwise have stayed at home. After the war the men have returned and demanded their old jobs back. In both the United States and Britain this has been a time of ethnic conflict, and old rules have been revived to limit the employment of married women.

Discrimination by employers should be lowest when they have to compete with one another for scarce labour. This is most apparent when they are competing for scarce talent. An example often cited is that of baseball teams in the USA. Prior to the 1950s baseball in the United States was racially segregated. There was a white league in which talented players were transferring at prices of $100 000 and more. There was a black league which included players of comparable talent who had never attracted transfer fees of more than $15 000 because the rich white teams would not bid for them. A man named Bill Veeck succeeded in buying a team called the Cleveland Indians which he began to fill with outstanding black players. Some members of the white public would not support teams with black players so they lost some revenue as a result, but with more star players non-discriminating teams won more matches and attracted spectators on this account. Economists have calculated that a team willing to employ four such black players among a 25 player team could increase its income by about $200 000 a year. This was a cost that was being borne by those which discriminated, and eventually it became too great for teams anxious to retain their places in the leagues. Nearly five years after the colour bar had been broken, many had desegregated though more than half were still holding out. Even in a situation as competitive as this it took time to overturn an uneconomic practice.

Since the elimination of discrimination can so rarely be secured by competitive pressures alone, progress towards this goal has to depend upon the introduction of formal controls, backed by law and the sorts of sanction an employer can use to ensure that orders are obeyed. One of these controls (to be discussed in Chapter 5) is the monitoring of appointments and promotions to see whether the decisions favour any particular class of persons to a disproportionate extent. Monitoring may be unnecessary in a highly competitive situation because there is no secret about whether a baseball team is winning matches, an entertainer is drawing an audience or a restaurant is making a profit. In few sectors of the economy do competitive pressures reach as far down as in entertainment. Government departments and other bureaucratic organizations are not subject to a similar consumer discipline. If a local government official is giving disproportionately more jobs, houses or licenses to members of his or her own racial or gender group, no one, including the official may know this, unless appropriate records are kept. The organization will not be incurring any costs as a result of the discrimination, so formal controls are all the more important.

Changes in the economy

Supply and demand vary from one individual to another and also in aggregate. Women and ethnic minority workers are employed disproportionately in certain sectors of the economy. In the European Union (EU) over three-quarters of female but only one half of male employees work in the service sector. This may have come about because the supply of female labour is directed more towards this sector, because there is less discrimination against them in it, or because of an interaction between the two. Yet the prevalence of gender-related job expectations can become more important when the structure of the economy changes. Six out of every ten additional jobs created in Europe between 1985 and 1990 went to women entering or returning to the labour market. This was possible because the service sector was expanding. Over the past 20 years women's share of jobs in this sector has grown at twice the men's rate.

Ethnic minority workers have settled disproportionately in the European manufacturing towns that experienced a labour shortage in the 1960s. In the 1980s the level of employment in manufacturing dropped, with negative consequences in Britain for Pakistani, Bangladeshi and West Indian groups in the West Midlands and the North, but the circumstances of some other minority groups, notably the Chinese and the Indians, improved over the decade because they were employed to a greater extent in the service sector and were more often self-employed. Variations in levels of education also played a part here.

The removal of trade barriers between the countries of the EU and changes in agreements governing international trade will have further implications. The textile industry in Europe (in which many female and minority workers are employed) will be subjected to increased competition from low-wage economies. This may well lead to an increase in home-working, an activity involving women almost exclusively, and in conditions which can more easily permit exploitation. Stronger international competition will, in some countries, force reductions in the state sector, where again relatively more women are employed. Women are particularly affected by the lack of cheap transport and crêches, which makes them a less mobile workforce. When the economic outlook is uncertain employers are likely to rely more upon part-time workers. This may suit some women, but it is a weak rung on most career ladders and it can reinforce the male assumption that women workers are less interested in promotion.

Any argument that the state should regulate the economy so as to engineer equal proportions of men and women, blacks and whites, etc., in each sector and occupational level, would be unrealistic. There are bound to be variations, and as the structure of the economy changes some groups will be winners and others losers. This reinforces the argument for differentiating between disadvantage and discrimination. The losers will suffer disadvantage, but if their loss arises from changes of this kind it will not be as a result of discrimination.

Conclusion

Chapter 1 argued for defining discrimination objectively and distinguishing it from moral judgements about its justifiability. Chapter 2 has contended that it is essential to distinguish discrimination from the larger phenomenon of disadvantage, as this can be seen in patterns of gender and racial inequality. These patterns are the products of a great variety of causes, of which discrimination is but one. So the concept of discrimination has been presented as an *explanans* that is the more likely to be important when supply is high relative to demand and when the price mechanism is not used to relate the one to the other. In these circumstances it is difficult to measure the costs of discrimination and therefore the pressures to reduce it are lower.

3

Locating Discrimination

A figure showing that disproportionately fewer judges are female, or that disproportionately more of the people in prison are black, indicates a certain degree of disadvantage related to gender or race. If it is seen as the end of a process of selection, it is then necessary, looking backwards, to note the earlier stage which provided the basis for concluding that one figure was disproportionate to the other. It is also important to identify the proper comparator, the figure with which the comparison is to be made. Then it can be advisable, looking forwards, to consider whether under-representation of females among the judges will affect the work of the courts, or whether over-representation of blacks in the prisons will affect future states of society. Statistics of inequality are snapshots of complex and continuing processes.

No one can ascertain the extent to which disadvantage is the result of discrimination without first understanding the process which has produced it. Lawyers and prisoners are both recruited disproportionately from certain sections of the general population, and there are later selections which decide who goes up and who goes down. It is essential to understand how the system works before looking to see if it is operated in a manner that gives some an advantage at the expense of others. Actual patterns of disadvantage are constantly changing because the systems change, sometimes as a result of complaints that they have built-in biases. The student needs to examine the whole selective process in order to measure any discrimination within it. The examples used in this chapter are taken from experience in Britain, but they have been chosen to illustrate methods for examining the incidence of discrimination and it should be possible to use similar methods in most countries.

[Readers outside Britain may note that the legal system of England and Wales is different from that of Scotland; all three countries together constitute Great Britain; when Northern Ireland is added in, it becomes the United Kingdom of Great Britain and Northern Ireland, but, for the sake of simplicity, reference has been made here to 'Britain' even in some contexts in which 'United Kingdom' would be technically the more correct.]

University entrance

In Britain anyone wishing to obtain a place in a university completes a standard form obtainable from a body which for many years was known as the Universities Central Council for Admissions, and familiarly called UCCA. The applicant specified five courses (which might be at five different universities), supplied information about his or her educational qualifications, and passed the form to a referee (usually the head teacher of a school), who provided an assessment of the applicant's merits and likely success in any forthcoming examinations, and then sent the form to UCCA headquarters. Though names may change, the more important consideration is that some universities and some courses are in greater demand than others; knowledge of this affects supply, in that candidates do not waste one of their five options applying for a course if they think they have no chance of obtaining a place. Many applicants are given advice about their chances at school.

UCCA photocopied the forms and sent copies to the universities listed, where they were distributed to the persons appointed as selectors. These picked out those they considered the best candidates and made them offers of places, either unconditional offers or offers conditional upon particular examination grades. Sometimes they called candidates for interview. Some offers were accepted, others declined. It was, and is, a highly competitive system with the selectors trying to get the best students before some other university got them, and the applicants trying to get into the most favoured courses. Sometimes the selectors erred by filling their places too quickly, sometimes they set their standards too high and were left with vacancies.

The pressure of well-qualified applicants chasing a limited number of places is exemplified in medicine. For reasons which will be explained shortly, this chapter begins with the St George's Hospital Medical School in London. In the mid-1980s they were receiving over 2 000 applications for 150 places; about 25 per cent of all applicants were selected for interview, and of these about 70 per cent were offered places. As the selection process was time-consuming, an attempt had been made to save time by the use of a computer program. The doctor who developed it wished to reduce inconsistencies in the decisions reached by him and his fellow selectors. He observed the decisions of the selectors over a number of years, noted the characteristics of the applicants who were offered places, and developed a program which would mimic the judgements of the selectors. After a test had showed that the results achieved by using the program correlated at a 90 to 95 per cent level with the decisions actually reached, the program was used to decide which applicants should be called for interview.

At much the same time two doctors elsewhere were worried about possible bias in admissions. A study of over 1 300 applicants to medical schools in 1981 found that 42 per cent of UK nationals with European surnames obtained admission compared with 31 per cent of UK nationals with non-European names; they found that this could not be explained by any differences in qualifications or the point in the cycle at which they applied. Two other doctors, with posts at St George's, studied admissions to the eleven London medical schools and found both that the proportion of non-national students varied from 5 to 16 per cent, and that this variation correlated strongly with the variation in the proportion of women students. St George's had the second highest proportion of non-European students. Then one of them discovered by chance that the computer program operated on a discriminatory basis when ranking candidates for interview. Males were ranked slightly higher than females and 'Caucasians' higher than 'non-Caucasians', so that around 10 per cent of applicants who would otherwise have been called for interview were not called beause they were female or from a minority ethnic group. Once this was discovered, use of the program was stopped. The School set up an inquiry, and the Commission for Racial Equality made use of its findings for its own investigation, the results of which were published in a report which has been used for this account.

Those who were responsible for selecting applicants for interview were not aware that they were discriminating on grounds of sex and race, either at the time the program was used, or, presumably, before it was introduced. They were not excluding all women, or all non-Europeans. It was simply that persons in particular categories had different chances of success and the differences could be expressed statistically. Why was this? Not long ago many British medical schools had a preference for male applicants, either because the selectors were men who thought that men made better doctors, or because the selectors thought that many female doctors would cease practising medicine at least for a time in order to care for children, and that therefore it was a better use of public resources to train males. At one stage many medical schools reckoned to admit no more than 33 per cent of female students, but such quotas have been abandoned.

This discussion of university entrance permits a preliminary answer to the question of how to locate discrimination. By comparing the numbers, qualifications and social characteristics of applicants with the numbers offered places, it is possible to point to any discrepancy which cannot be ascribed to factors proper to the selection process, but which are associated with the gender, race or disability of applicants. The outcome strongly suggests discrimination without identifying who was responsible. Since sex discrimination so often stems from customary notions of what is appropriate to the male and female roles, such evidence may be all that is needed as a basis for anti-discrimination policies. Conceptions of racial differences are more complicated than the male-female difference, and the causes of racial discrimination are often less straightforward. Sex discrimination is less important than racial discrimination in fields such as those of criminal justice and housing, so in seeking to locate racial discrimination it is necessary to go much further.

Nearly all those applying for places in British medical schools have British qualifications, but when someone does not, it can be troublesome to discover the relative value of an alternative qualification. The unfamiliar is seen as risky, and reactions may be governed by unjustified expectations. Thus a study of employment opportunities conducted in London in 1966–67 mentioned two examples: 'The manager of one company explained why he had rejected an applicant for a secretarial post – "Asian . . . a charming woman, 40-ish, capable, been here a long time. Her English was good although not her first language. But we both felt [he and the personnel officer] that if she got excited her English would fall down".' The second example related to a Lieutenant-Colonel of Engineers and a graduate of Rangoon University, of whom it was said 'He had Sapper experience in the post-war Indian Army. Hard to judge whether he was any good . . . it was not the British Army, after all', a comment surely ignorant of standards in the Indian Army at the time in question (Rose *et al.* 1969: 321). Research which follows through a sample of applicants and collects the selectors' views of their suitability, can usefully assemble information about selectors' perceptions. These can be crucial, but it is a time-consuming method of enquiry.

Criminal justice

The example of discrimination in the allocation of university places has been treated first because it describes a process with which many student readers will be familiar, but in some respects the criminal justice system would provide a better example. The university entrance process is more complicated than it has so far been represented, because there are possibilities of discrimination in the writing of referees' reports, in the conduct of interviews, and there is what is called the 'clearing' process at the end when there is a scramble to fill unanticipated vacancies. Such discrimination as occurs is likely to accumulate from minor biases. The criminal justice system is extremely complex because it is regulated by a massive body of written law which is intended to provide for every possible eventuality though, inevitably, it leaves much scope for the exercise of personal discretion. Because of that discretion, and the nature of the decisons that have to be made, there are situations in which highly discriminatory decisions may be taken without proper accountability.

At its simplest, the process starts with police officers stopping people in the street for questioning, arresting some, taking them to the police station where they may be either charged or released, kept in custody or given bail, then brought before a court, allowed or denied court bail – with or without conditions, tried in a lower or a higher court, found guilty or not guilty, and made subject to sentences that vary greatly in their severity, from a fine to a long period of imprisonment.

Discrimination is more likely to occur in the criminal justice system than in university entrance. University selectors are competing for the best students. If they have a preference for students of any particular kind it is likely to be one factor among many and probably not a high priority. In medicine, for example, they are selecting people to join their own profession, people who, if they are not already of a socio-economic status similar to that of the selectors, will acquire that status. In criminal justice, however, the decisions are taken by persons responsible for law and order who are dealing with others who have apparently offended, so any factor of gender or race is caught up in a relation in which ostensibly moral people are dealing with people suspected of illegality; the social and moral components may reinforce any disposition to discriminate.

Study of the prison statistics (Home Office 1991a) must raise questions about the possibility of discrimination. In Britain in 1990, persons with origins in the minority ethnic groups accounted for about 5.8 per cent of the total population but 18.2 per cent of the prison population. Persons of West Indian or West African origin accounted for 1.1 per cent of the total population, but 11.2 per cent of the prison population. More striking still, 24 per cent of the female prison population were of West Indian or West African origin. Crude figures of this kind can be misleading. It is always necessary to remember that a great deal of crime is committed by young men. Immigrant groups often include a high proportion of young men and relatively few old people. But even after correcting for differences in age distributions, these and other figures indicate that in Britain blacks are more involved in criminal proceedings than whites, and Asians rather less involved than either. An appreciable number of the imprisoned black women were foreign nationals who had been convicted for the importation of illegal drugs, an offence which attracts an above-average sentence. Figures on the total prison population can convey a different impression from figures on the numbers of persons sentenced to imprisonment, because the former total is sensitive to any increase in the number of persons serving long sentences.

Ethnic groups are distinguished by the ways in which their culture differs from that of other groups, and they will therefore have their characteristic forms of deviance. Crimes against the person and 'street crime' have a higher visibility than tax evasion or commercial fraud. They arouse more concern and result in more public proceedings. Sociologists have described the creation of subcultures of drug-users and of youths who take cars in order to race them. There can equally be subcultures of persons from a particular ethnic group with a distinctive pattern of criminality, and if, like street crime, it is frequently repeated, it makes a big impact upon the figures. Thus notices were posted by the police in south London early in 1991 stating: 'About 60 people are responsible for 90 per cent of the street crime in Brixton' and appealing for the help of the public in bringing them to book. The notice did not say that many of the 60 people were black, but that may well have been so, and, given that it is harder for blacks to obtain employment and that they are subject to more deprivation, it should not occasion surprise if that were to be the case. Such considerations must be taken into account before inferring that racial discrimination is the prime factor in the relative over-representation of blacks in the prison population.

Important decisions are taken before an offender reaches the court. Studies have found that relatively more black people are stopped in the street for police questioning but fewer are charged with an offence as a result; this suggests that the police more frequently hold unjustified suspicions of blacks. Having been charged, some offenders are given bail, and this is a second point at which unjustified suspicion may have an effect.

One of the best studies so far published of what happens thereafter was an analysis of decisions in London in 1983 (Walker 1989: 353–67). This found that more blacks than whites were refused bail by both the police and the courts. Since they will have been held in prison while awaiting trial this will have contributed to the over-representation of blacks in the prison population. The London study was of white, black and Asian suspects divided into two age categories: those aged between 17–20 years, and those between 21–25 years. This is important to the analysis of discrimination, because in some cases a difference suggesting discrimination was found for the one age category but not the other. Taking both categories together, it looks as if any discrimination was relatively small. The most important findings were that slightly more blacks were not tried in the magistrates' courts but were committed to the Crown Court (which has greater sentencing powers). In Crown Court more blacks were acquitted and more blacks were sentenced to imprisonment. The figures do not indicate what proportion of blacks were committed to the Crown Court because the magistrates thought their offences merited heavier sentences, and in what proportion because the offenders themselves elected trial in the higher court. The greater availability of legal aid to persons of low income is a possible factor in defendants' decisions, but is unlikely to have been of more than marginal significance.

That more blacks were acquitted in Crown Court suggests that their prosecutions were based on weaker evidence than those of comparable whites. That more blacks were made subject to custodial sentences (prison or youth custody) might be because their offences were the more serious, but other studies have found that black prisoners have fewer previous convictions recorded against them, suggesting that racial discrimination has influenced sentencing. There are other factors, too, which have been omitted from this summary. One alternative to a custodial sentence is for the offender to be placed on probation. At one stage it appeared as if probation officers were less likely to recommend this course, possibly because of bias, but also possibly because they as white people felt that they were less likely to be able to strike up the right kind of relationship with a young black probationer. The increase in the number of black probation officers may have eased this difficulty.

More recent research on the sentencing of offenders in the Crown Court in the West Midlands has estimated that four-fifths of the over-representation of black males in the prison population has arisen from the larger number of blacks convicted in the Crown Court, and one-fifth of it from what happened when they were before the court (whether or not they were eligible for a lesser sentence for pleading guilty, and the nature of their sentence). The percentages sentenced to custody were: whites, 48.8; blacks, 56.6; Asians; 39.6. After allowance was made for the seriousness of the offence for which the men were sentenced, the black-white differential was 2.5 per cent (Hood 1992: 179, 184). Perhaps more important, the study also found differences in the severity of sentencing from one town to another. After calculating a 'prob-ability of custody score' based on factual information in the case papers, the research workers found no black-white differential in the sentencing in the Birmingham Crown Court but a 30 per cent differential in Dudley. Since the research workers were not permitted to interview the judges, explanations of the difference remain conjectural but it is the judges who have to account for their practice.

The study by Walker also highlighted the extent to which decisions taken at one stage affected what happened at subsequent stages. If the police gave a suspect bail, so in 99 per cent of cases did the magistrates, but about half of those whom the police held in custody were subsequently given bail by the courts, perhaps with conditions. When the police decision to withhold bail was compared with the final verdict, there was no great difference as between whites, blacks and Asians, which would suggest that any police bias at this stage can have been only small. This summary should at least outline the complexities of the task of locating discrimination in a criminal justice system and the need for care in selecting the appropriate comparator.

Housing

Selection for university entrance and decisions in the criminal justice system can be represented as stages in a linear process. Discrimination in housing markets is more complex because of the division between the private and the public sectors, and then the further divisions within these. In Britain in 1988 64 per cent of households owned the dwellings in which they lived (24 per cent owned them outright and 40 per cent were paying off mortgages they had taken out in order to buy them); 26 were renting council houses from a municipality, while 8 per cent were renting privately or from a housing association. The first decision taken by a couple planning to enter the housing market is whether they will aim at the private or the public sector. One small-scale study (Ineichen 1981) found couples who were similar in all the relevant respects except that they had made different decisions in this regard. Those who were aiming at owner-occupation found that it was best to delay having children and for the woman to remain in employment as long as possible while they saved money. Those who were aiming at a council house found that it was best to start having a family soon while staying with the parents of one of the couple so that they accumulated 'points' that would take them towards the top of the queue. If they lived in poor circumstances so that they could get a medical certificate recommending their rehousing on grounds of health, this too was an advantage. So couples who had initially been similar, became more and more dissimilar as they progressed.

Couples with an ethnic minority background who sought housing in the private sector could well have encountered racial discrimination. In 1989 the Commission for Racial Equality conducted an experimental investigation of accommodation agencies, landlords and landladies, and small hotels and guest houses, in 13 localities throughout Britain (CRE 1990). In each locality they trained eight testers, four male, four female, one man and one woman being either Afro-Caribbean or African and another Asian, so as to constititute four carefully matched pairs of persons who differed from one another in no important respect other than their ethnic origins.

A minority tester visited an accommodation agency and asked for written details about the number and location of properties available for rent of a particular kind. The white tester followed 15 to 20 minutes later and asked for the same details. The agency was considered to have failed the test if,

1 the first tester was given fewer details than the second, or
2 was directed towards areas in which there was a substantial ethnic minority population, or
3 the agency asked enquirers to complete a form which asked for the enquirer's nationality and it was admitted to the white tester that this was included to enable the agency to comply with discriminatory instructions from landlords and landladies, or
4 derogatory comments were made about multi-racial areas and the white tester was steered away from them, or
5 the first tester was refused registration but not the second tester.

If the first test was 'failed', or the result was inconclusive, it was repeated the following day using a different pair of testers.

Possible racial discrimination by landlords and landladies was tested over the telephone. A tester with a pronounced Afro-Caribbean or Asian accent telephoned to request details of an advertised property. If he or she was told that the accommodation had already been taken, a white tester of the same sex telephoned five to ten minutes later. If he or she was told that the accommodation was still available, this was taken as evidence of discrimination. In the case of small hotels and guest houses, the ethnic minority tester visited or telephoned to ask if a room would be available on a particular date. If the first tester was given a negative answer, a white tester then visited or telephoned.

In one locality in the west of London, 45 per cent of accommodation agencies failed the test three times running, but the national average (of 209 agencies) showed a 20.5 per cent probability of discrimination. For landlords and landladies the incidence was 5.5 per cent and for small hotels and guest houses 5 per cent.

The report on this research provides some examples of what happened. One of them reads:

K, an ethnic minority female tester, made the usual enquiry [of an agency] about what was available. The agent took out a list and

proceeded to telephone six landlords/landladies to check on availability; he was apparently told that all six had 'gone'. He then offered
three addresses, all in multi-racial areas and not those she had
requested. K left the agency with the impression that he had made
every effort to find something suitable and had spent a long time
trying to help. Ten minutes later, L, her white partner, made the
same enquiry. Straightaway, the agent gave her five addresses in the
areas and price range requested. Clearly, some agencies were ready
to go to extraordinary lengths in discriminating against particular
clients.

(CRE 1990: 31)

In instances like this the minority testers would never have realized
that they had been discriminated against had they not been followed
by their white partners. It taught them that discrimination was much
more widespread than they had suspected. This made it all the more
important that, at the end of each day, 'debriefing sessions' were
conducted. As the report explains, although the ethnic minority
testers often felt that they were well-prepared for possible discrimination, most were to some extent traumatized by their experiences.
They could feel angry and rejected, while their white partners,
exposed to first-hand experience of the differences in treatment,
could feel guilty and ashamed. The debriefing sessions brought
these emotions out into the open, helping to restore the confidence
and self-esteem of people who had been subjected to a dehumaniz-
ing experience.

Discrimination in the housing market occurs when someone is
refused housing on racial grounds. It also occurs when someone, on
these grounds, is offered housing on less favourable terms. A study
in the Manchester suburbs in the mid-1970s (Fenton 1976) concluded that Asian purchasers were paying about 5 per cent more for
the houses they bought. It would seem as if many vendors did not
wish to sell to purchasers of a different ethnic group and that estate
agents also tried to 'preserve the character' of certain neighbourhoods. So minority purchasers had to spend longer searching for
properties and were paying a 5 per cent colour tax when they did so.
Research workers in the United States have found that blacks pay
between 10 and 20 per cent more than whites for comparable
housing; higher-income blacks seeking high quality houses may
have to pay an even higher premium in some areas (Yinger *et al*.
1979: 108).

A study of the allocation of council housing in London (Smith

1977) supported the conclusion that the main feature of this market was the excess of demand over supply caused by prior central government policies. These, by seeking to control rents, had caused those who previously rented out their properties privately to sell them instead to prospective owner-occupiers. The number of owner-occupied dwellings in the United Kingdom more than doubled between 1961 and 1989 and is higher than in most other industrial countries.

Because of the excess demand for council housing, those responsible for allocating dwellings had to operate a rationing scheme. Applicants were divided into three main categories, each of which followed a distinctive route through the allocation process:

- those on the waiting list;
- those who had to be rehoused immediately (or 'decanted') because they were living in houses that were about to be demolished as part of the process of urban renewal;
- homeless families, who had a claim in law upon the local authority to find them somewhere to live.

The supply of housing for allocation was also divided into three main categories:

- newly-built, and therefore desirable houses, maisonettes or flats (in that order of popular preference);
- vacant properties that had been built earlier by the council;
- vacant properties bought by the council as part of urban renewal but not yet due for demolition (though possibly in a poor state of repair).

When matching demand to supply, the authorities had to give a high time priority to homeless families, but they were given a low priority in the queue for the most desirable properties. Families displaced by 'clearance' (or urban renewal) were given a high priority in respect of both timing and quality of dwelling offered. Waiting list applicants had a low time but a high quality priority (Smith 1977: 246–7).

The points at which discrimination could occur were chiefly:

1 eligibility (legal action had to be taken to counter the claim that people who had left their homes in Bangladesh in order to come to London had made themselves intentionally homeless and therefore ineligible);

2 in the allocation of points;
3 in the allocation of families to dwellings of an unsuitable size; and
4 in the process by which families were matched with localities of varying desirability.

(It can happen that the existing tenants are angered when families who do not live up to their norms of respectability are moved into their locality, and they can complain vigorously about this; so the procedure is for a housing visitor to call upon applicant families and form an impression of their housekeeping standards in order that they may be allocated to localities matching their standards.) Inequalities also result because applicants make ill-advised choices. They may bid for less desirable localities in the belief that they will not be offered better ones. Some applicants are in a stronger position, or are more determined, and hold out for the localities they want, or, having secured a dwelling, later apply for a transfer or arrange an exchange. An earlier study (Smith 1977: 262) suggested that native applicants might be better at looking after their own interests in these respects than were immigrants. It is therefore clear that many forms of inequality can result without there being any deliberate policy of discrimination.

A local authority is nevertheless under an obligation to guard against discrimination and to see that allocations are fair. Some have not been conscientious in this regard, and this was the background to an investigation of housing policies in the Borough of Hackney, London, carried out by the Commission for Racial Equality in 1978–82 (CRE 1984). It found that of a balanced sample of dwellings which, over a 12-month period, were allocated to families on the waiting list, 79 per cent of the houses, 64 per cent of the maisonettes and 46 per cent of the flats were allocated to whites, compared to figures of 21, 36 and 54 per cent allocations to ethnic minority families. This difference could have arisen from differences in family size, but a further check showed that whites in every category of family size did better. More whites were allocated to the newer and more desirable properties and more of them obtained dwellings on the ground floor or first floor level, although they did not include any more pensioners or families with small children who might have required a low floor level. Those who obtain housing by transfer resemble, to some extent, waiting-list applicants, except that in this particular study it transpired that most of the transfers were on grounds of overcrowding, and it looked as if non-whites living in overcrowded dwellings had more difficulty obtaining transfers. The research team next looked at allocations to the two least desirable housing estates to see if they could find any non-racial factors which might contribute to these differences (such as any history of rent arrears), but they found none and therefore concluded that discrimination must have occurred.

Examining the other two routes through which applicants obtained housing, they found that, among those who had to be moved (or 'decanted'), a larger proportion of whites were given dwellings in the newly-built category while a larger proportion of ethnic minority families were allocated to vacant properties acquired by the Council. Of the homeless applicants, more of the whites than of the ethnic minority groups were allocated houses. None of the white families was given a dwelling above 5-floor level, unlike the ethnic minority families, two of which had a child under the age of five and should therefore have been given a flat lower down in accordance with Council policy. Like the other differences reported here, these differences were statistically significant and no non-racial explanations were found. Because of deficiencies in the records, the study could not identify any particular stage in the process as being primarily responsible for the differential outcome. The way in which the housekeeping standards of applicants were recorded by the housing visitors was unsystematic and may have been influenced by racial stereotyping but the allocators seemed not to rely very much upon these assessments. After digesting these findings, the Commission notified the Council that they would be issuing a non-discrimination notice, and that to comply with it the Council would have to keep records of the ethnic origins of applicants and of their allocations, to provide training for their staff, and to keep their arrangements under review in order to eliminate discrimination.

Employment

Experimental studies in Britain employing 'situation testing' have found significant levels of racial discrimination in the job market. An applicant for a post may telephone to enquire about it. The person at the other end of the telephone may detect that the enquirer speaks with a particular accent, or has a distinctive choice of words, and from this conclude that the enquirer is a particular sort of person. Equally, if someone applies by post, any information given about the applicant's place of birth may make a difference. A series of studies (summarized in Banton 1988: 98–100) has submitted job applications in the names of persons whose qualifications were similar but who appear to be of different national or ethnic origin to see if this influences decisions about whom to call for interview. They have discovered that white employers in Britain operate with a scale of preference in which Britons are preferred to Australians, who in turn are preferred to French people, then Africans, West Indians, Indians and Pakistanis. It has been found that at least one-third of employers discriminate against either West Indians or Asians, and at least one in five discriminates against both.

Experimental methods have been of primary use for measuring the incidence of racial discrimination, but have not been much used for the study of discrimination on grounds of gender. In this field there has been a greater reliance on aggregate statistics of the numbers of men and women employed at different levels. All employers will have records which indicate whether the employees are male or female, but without ethnic monitoring they will not have comparable statistics that could throw light on any discrimination on racial grounds.

Causes

Evidence of disadvantage may be traced back to discrimination, which may in turn be traced to taste, risk and profit. These too have their causes. Peoples' tastes for associating with those similar to or dissimilar from those with whom they grew up may reflect a psychological disposition either to conform to their conditioning or to react against it. The perception, that relations with strangers entail greater risks than relations with more familiar people, is in part a reflection of experience. Whether a particular situation makes it possible to profit from discrimination leads back to an economic analysis.

Causes and effects link up in a chain. To study discrimination is to examine one link in it defined by strict criteria as to whether a particular decision was taken on a prohibited ground. In this respect discrimination resembles a crime, in that the person who acted on the basis of that ground is responsible for what he or she did and its consequences. Sometimes, of course, people's actions spring not from their own wishes but from the orders they have been given or the pressure to which they are subject, and in these cases their responsibility may be diminished. This has been a problem with trials for war crimes in which the accused has claimed that he or she had no alternative but to obey an order given. When a pattern of discrimination stretches right through a society affecting decisions at all levels, it is often likened not to a crime but to a sickness. Racism and sexism have sometimes been defined in ways that strengthen the resemblance to a pathology. The danger with such definitions is that they may weaken individual accountability and exculpate people who ought to be punished or reprimanded. Since the words racism and sexism are so frequently used it may be better to try to reserve them for the more pathological situations in order to preserve the conception of discrimination as crime-like be-haviour for which individuals must be held accountable.

Conclusion

Discriminators are often unconscious of their own discrimination. They have long assumed that some kinds of people are less well suited than others to certain positions. It may be difficult to establish that a particular person was treated less favourably on grounds of race or gender but statistics covering a sequence of decisions may show that there has been a tendency to discriminate. This chapter has outlined the kinds of methods sociologists have developed for locating and measuring the incidence of discrimi-nation.

4

Protections from Discrimination

The best protections against discrimination are those in the hearts of people who believe discrimination to be wrong. Yet even such people do not always perceive differential treatment to be discriminatory, and may think that particular circumstances constitute a justifiable exception, especially when their personal interests pull them in that direction. Though formal controls are a second best line of protection, experience shows them to be necessary. This chapter will outline some of the main protections in international law intended to improve protection and the measures introduced in some states.

State obligations

Whereas the covenant of the League of Nations was agreed (in 1919) between 'the High Contracting Parties' (i.e., the states), the Charter of the United Nations (1945) began 'We the peoples of the United Nations, determined to save succeeding generations from the scourge of war . . . and to reaffirm faith in fundamental human rights . . .' This suggested a shift towards the view that peoples ought to come before states, even if in practice the UN has found no way of ensuring that they do. The Charter asserted that protection of those rights was seen as necessary 'to strengthen universal peace'.

The UN Charter lists four classes of persons to be protected from discrimination, and, as was mentioned in Chapter 1, the Universal Declaration of Human Rights (UDHR) extended this list. That Declaration is the foundation for the International Bill of Human Rights, but the drafting of the Bill was delayed by different views about priorities. The UDHR proclaimed certain rights as the 'inalienable rights of all members of the human family', in line with the Western view of civil rights as preceding the formation of states (the US Declaration of Independence avers that it is to secure such pre-existing rights that 'Governments are instituted among Men'). Countries of the Eastern bloc believed that the Western philosophy had been responsible for the misery of the working classes in capitalist countries, and therefore thought the state should confer upon its citizens rights they might not otherwise have. They wished to stress economic rights (the view that human rights begin after breakfast), where Westerners were chiefly concerned with civil rights (the view that human rights begin in the police station). As a result, two texts were prepared, the International Covenant on Economic, Social and Cultural Rights (ICESCR), and the International Covenant on Civil and Political Rights (ICCPR). These, together with two optional protocols now make up the International Bill. The covenants take the form of treaties which impose legal obligations upon those states that accede to them. They came into force in 1976.

Other action of a comparable kind was taken outside the UN. The International Labour Office (ILO) adopted in 1958 the Discrimination (Employment and Occupation) Convention no. 111. Regional bodies (such as the Council of Europe) have also played an important part in the human rights movement, establishing the European Convention for the Protection of Human Rights and Fundamental Freedoms, the American Convention on Human Rights and the African Charter on Human and Peoples' Rights. The European Convention states in Article 14 that its rights shall be secured 'without discrimination on any ground such as sex, race, colour, language, religion, political or other opinion, national or social origin, association with a national minority, property, birth or other status'. The American Convention has in its Article 1(1) a similar provision but with no reference to national minorities. The African Charter in its Article 2 lists 12 protected classes, 'ethnic group' being among them.

At the United Nations, the usual procedure has been to seek support first for a declaration of principles (like the UDHR) and then to try and give it an acceptable legal form in a covenant or convention. Progress has been more rapid in some fields than others. Conventions are now in force against Genocide (entered into effect 1951), Racial Discrimination (1969), Apartheid (1976), Discrimination against Women (1981), Apartheid in Sports (1985),

Table 1   Acceptance of international obligations

In this table an x in a column indicates that by 1996 the state had ratified the international convention; xx indicates that it had both ratified the convention against racial discrimination and agreed that those within its jurisdiction might petition an international tribunal if they considered that the government had failed to furnish the promised protections; s indicates that the state had signed the convention but that this had not been ratified by the legislature and given legal force; r indicates, for the ILO convention, that while the state had not ratified, it submitted reports on matters covered by the convention.

ICERD stands for the International Convention on the Elimination of All Forms of Racial Discrimination; CEDAW for the Convention on the Elimination of All Forms of Discrimination against Women; ILO 111 for the Discrimination (Employment and Occupation) Convention no. 111 of the International Labour Office.

State	ICERD	CEDAW	ILO 111
Australia	xx	x	x
Austria	x	x	x
Bangladesh	x	x	x
Belgium	x	x	x
Canada	x	x	x
China	x	x	r
Denmark	xx	x	x
France	xx	x	x
Germany	x	x	x
Greece	x	x	x
India	x	x	x
Ireland	s	x	r
Italy	xx	x	x
Japan	x	x	r
Netherlands	xx	x	x
New Zealand	x	x	x
Norway	xx	x	x
Pakistan	x	x	x
Portugal	x	x	x
Russia	xx	x	x
Spain	x	x	x
Sweden	xx	x	x
Switzerland	x	s	x
United Kingdom	x	x	r
United States of America	x	s	r

Torture (1987) and the Rights of the Child (1990). A convention has been adopted on the Rights of Migrant Workers and their Families which has not yet entered into effect. A declaration was adopted in 1981 on the Elimination of All Forms of Intolerance and Discrimination Based on Religion or Belief, and another in 1992 on the rights of persons belonging to national or ethnic, religious and linguistic minorities. A draft declaration on the rights of indigenous peoples is in preparation.

Table 1 offers, for a selected list of states, an indication of which of them have acceded to the conventions dealing with discrimination on grounds of race and sex. Some states, like the USA, are slow to accept a legal obligation to the international community but nevertheless take action in conformity with the international standard, perhaps because of pressure from their own citizens.

According to Article 1 of ICERD,

> the term 'racial discrimination' shall mean any distinction, exclusion, restriction or preference based on race, colour, descent, or national or ethnic origin which has the purpose or effect of nullifying or impairing the recognition, enjoyment or exercise, on an equal footing, of human rights and fundamental freedoms in the political, economic, social, cultural or any other field of public life.

It then goes on to make certain exceptions, such as that which says that the Convention shall not apply to distinctions made by a state between citizens and non-citizens. Thus a state may discriminate lawfully when it decides who may become a citizen.

At national and local levels legal protections have been extended to classes other than those included in the convention. In Britain, for example, the legislation against racial discrimination covers both national origin (i.e., the group into which a person is born) and nationality (i.e., the state in which a person currently has citizenship). Extension of the legal protections to prohibit discrimination on grounds of age, disability and sexual orientation is more contentious and will be considered later. However, two contrary arguments may be noted at this point. On the one hand it is maintained that many classes of persons can be the victims of discrimination and that therefore all should be listed. On the other hand it is said, first, that it is wrong to include a group unless its members are willing to identify themselves so that effective protections can be arranged, and, second, that no list can include all possible victim groups. Persons with AIDS might be added as such a group, and then later persons with some new medical condition. To include one without mentioning another may suggest that the exclusion was deliberate (*inclusio unus est exclusio alterius* is the legal maxim). So it may be better to rely not on a list of classes but on a positive statement, such as one in the author's university's employment policy which says that it 'will operate selection and promotion criteria and procedures which are designed in accordance with good employment practice to ensure that individuals are selected, promoted, trained and treated on the basis of the job requirements and their relevant aptitudes, skills and abilities'.

Just as there are protected classes of persons, so there are protected fields of activity. The ICERD requires state parties to guarantee the right of everyone to equality before the law in the enjoyment of rights in 'the political, economic, social, cultural, or any other field of *public* life' (italics added). There is therefore a distinction drawn between public and private life which is not found in the Convention on the Elimination of Discrimination Against Women. Its definition of discrimination against women parallels the other convention's definition of racial discrimination, reading:

> For the purposes of the present Convention, the term 'discrimination against women' shall mean any distinction, exclusion or restriction made on the basis of sex which has the effect or purpose of impairing or nullifying the recognition, enjoyment or exercise by women, irrespective of their marital status, on a basis of equality of men and women, of human rights and fundamental freedoms in the political, economic, social, cultural, civil or any other field.

There is no restriction to public life.

The failure to appreciate that anti-discrimination provisions are restricted to particular protected fields has been one of the prime sources of opposition to legislation against discrimination. Thus in 1883, the United States Supreme Court ruled unconstitutional a federal statute forbidding the exclusion or segregation of blacks, on the grounds of race alone, in public transport and places of public resort. It was said:

> It would be running the slavery argument into the ground to make it apply to every act of discrimination which a person may see fit to make as to the guests he will entertain, or as to the people he will take into his coach, or cab or car, or admit to his concert or theatre, or deal with in other matters of intercourse or business.

The federal act forbade the owners of railroads, hotels and theatres, that is, commercial enterprises, to discriminate in their commercial transactions, but the court equated these transactions with 'social intercourse' between a 'person' and his 'guests'. This distinction between public and private life will be considered further in Chapter 5. Here it should be noted that the protection of women's rights must entail regulation of relations within the family. Protections from racial discrimination can be restricted to public life, but even here there will need to be exceptions.

In Britain a person may make a bequest to a charity specifically for members of that person's own ethnic group. The Indian Workers' Association can reject English or Pakistani applicants for membership. An employer may discriminate racially where 'being of a particular racial group is a genuine occupational qualification for a job' (paralleling the exception in US law for a 'bona fide occupational qualification' and in Canadian law for a 'bona fide occupational requirement'); it can be applied to a theatrical role, a photographic model, a waiter in an 'ethnic' restaurant, or a social worker providing personal services to persons of a particular racial group. It can be lawful to discriminate in providing services to meet the special needs of racial groups in regard to education, training and welfare. These are all examples of lawful discrimination, permissible under national legislation. It is necessary to specify such exceptions, and to permit them to be challenged in court, because otherwise reasonable actions would be prohibited by the legal definition of racial discrimination. The international convention does not go into such fine detail but the committee which monitors compliance with the Convention would draw the attention of the UN General Assembly were any state party to make exceptions contrary to the spirit of the Convention.

Constitutions and statutes

States can fulfil their obligations in ways appropriate to their own legal systems. In some states, once the government signs a treaty or accepts some international obligation, that action immediately enters into effect in its domestic law. In other states domestic legislation has to be enacted in order to give effect to the treaty. In very many states, protection against discrimination is provided in the constitution and is subject to interpretation in constitutional law. In other states the protection has to be provided by a particular statute passed by the legislature.

An additional protection is provided when a state agrees that anyone within its jurisdiction who believes that he or she has not received a promised protection may petition an international tribunal. This is done when a state accedes to the first optional protocol of the ICCPR or makes a declaration under Article 14 of the ICERD (and gets an extra x in the first column of Table 1). A good example is offered by a Canadian case. Sandra Lovelace, a registered Maliseet Indian, lost her status as an Indian when she married a non-Indian, and could not get it back when the marriage ended. When she returned to live on the Maliseet reserve, she was threatened with eviction under the Canadian law relating to Indian reserves. Since Canada (unlike the USA and the UK) is a party to the first optional protocol to the ICCPR, Sandra Lovelace could petition the UN Human Rights Committee. The Committee enquired into her communication and issued an opinion that her rights under the minorities article of the covenant had been violated. Canada then amended her legislation. As readers will notice, this case could also have been regarded as touching on sex discrimination, since it was only an Indian woman who lost her Indian status on marrying a non-Indian.

In the United States of America the constitution adopted in 1789, together with subsequent amendments, details the rights of citizenship. There is no list of protected classes in the federal constitution. It is United States citizenship that is protected, and the due process clause forbids any discrimination by agencies of the federal government. Citizens also live in states belonging to the federation and are subject to the laws of those states. The federal constitution limits the powers of the constituent states. In the equal protection clause of article XIV it declares that no state may abridge the privileges of US citizens but, to cite just a single example, it took many decades for the federal Supreme Court to find that state legislation prohibiting inter-racial marriage was unconstitutional. In matters that cannot be regulated by states, such as inter-state transport and postal services, federal law obtains. Then there are particular anti-discrimination laws at both the federal and state levels.

From the time of the US Civil War (1861–65) there has been a succession of Civil Rights Acts, the most notable being that of 1964; this was directed at racial discrimination in places of public resort (like restaurants and sports stadia), at segregated facilities operated by local authorities in receipt of federal grants, and at job discrimination. It established an Equal Employment Opportunity Commission (EEOC) which could compel the attendance of witnesses and the production of documents; it could require records to be kept and reports to be made; it could conduct its own investigations and could get the courts to make orders. It was followed in the same year by a Voting Rights Act designed to discipline recalcitrant states and local authorities, and in 1968 by a further act prohibiting racial discrimination in private housing.

The Civil Rights Act, 1964, in Title VII at §703(a), states:

> It shall be an unlawful practice for an employer [of 15 or more persons] . . . to fail or refuse to hire . . . any individual . . . or discriminate with respect to his compensation, terms, conditions, or privileges of employment, because of such individual's race, color, religion, sex, or national origin . . .'

So discrimination on grounds of sex is covered in the same terms as discrimination on grounds of race. In the US, state prohibitions upon discrimination may be more extensive than federal prohibitions (thus in California the 'Unruh law' which forms Section 51 of the Civil Code prohibits discrimination in 'business establishments', so that cases have been brought – so far with little success – against private clubs which employ only males) but any organization which wishes to benefit from federal money can be obliged to meet federal standards. Thus in 1968 the Department of Labor started to require every contractor and sub-contractor for federal contracts to submit an affirmative action compliance programme showing what they were doing to utilize minority-group personnel. Since most universities and colleges benefited from federal money, they were greatly affected by such measures in the 1970s, but more recent court decisions have restricted the enforcement powers of federal agencies in this field.

As in the United States, British anti-discrimination law has been built up gradually. The first Race Relations Act, in 1965, prohibited discrimination in places of public resort and established the Race Relations Board to bring proceedings when complaints were registered. In 1968, partly because of an experimental study demonstrating the incidence of discrimination to be higher than almost eveyone had thought, the law was extended to cover employment, housing, education and advertising. In 1975 a Sex

Discrimination Act was passed, followed in the next year by a new Race Relations Act which abolished the Race Relations Board and allowed any complainant to seek a remedy through the industrial tribunals whose character and functions had been developed since 1965.

The nearest approach to affirmative action in British law is to be found in Sections 35, 37 and 38 of the Race Relations Act which make it lawful to afford training and comparable services to members of particular racial groups to enable them to compete on an equal basis with others for employment. This is referred to as 'positive action'. For example, some police forces which wished to increase the number of their black and Asian police officers, have mounted courses to help selected candidates, primarily blacks, who failed the entrance examination the first time. They have to reach the same standard as other recruits. There is no discrimination at the point of entry, as under quota provisions, but selected individuals are offered help to reach that standard.

The prohibition of racial discrimination is to be extended to Northern Ireland. Hitherto the British government has thought it necessary to prohibit discrimination there on grounds of gender, religion and political opinion, but not on grounds of race. This has had the paradoxical consequence that in London it has been unlawful to deny a Jewish man a job on the grounds of his ethnic origin, but not on the ground of his religion, whereas in Belfast it would be the other way round! The difficulty of distinguishing the grounds of discriminatory action is apparent in other parts of the world also. For example, if Israel discriminated against Arabs in expelling them from their land when it occupied the Golan Heights, did it treat them differently because they were Arabs or on grounds of national security? Can the two be separated in circumstances such as these?

The Treaty of Rome, which was one of the three treaties which led to the foundation of the European Union in 1967 (when its three precursors were merged), lays down in Article 119 the principle that men and women should receive equal pay for equal work. This has now been supplemented by five EU directives, on Equal Pay, Equal Treatment, two on Social Security and one on Self-Employment. The Treaty covers only sex discrimination, so there has been no opportunity to develop and issue directives on other forms of discrimination. Nevertheless, all European countries have prohibited racial discrimination either by some general provision in their constitution or by statute. In some states, e.g., Germany, the protections against discrimination by state institutions are much more comprehensive than those in the private sphere. In all of these states it is more difficult than in Britain for the victims of racial discrimination to gain access to tribunals able to adjudicate upon their grievance and there are doubts about the effectiveness with which the legal measures are implemented.

Purpose and effect

The international conventions against racial and sex discrimination both prohibit acts which are discriminatory in either purpose or effect. A major decision in developing laws against discriminatory effects was that of *Griggs v. Duke Power Company*, in which the US Supreme Court was faced with an employer who made appointments to certain posts conditional upon possession of a high school diploma or the passing of two tests. It could not be proved that the intention in imposing these conditions was discriminatory, but the black plaintiffs claimed that the condition was discriminatory in effect. The employer could not prove that either the diploma or the intelligence test bore a demonstrable relationship to successful performance of the jobs for which one or the other was required. The Supreme Court has stated that a primary objective of Title VII is to achieve equal employment opportunity and to remove barriers. It has distinguished between disparate treatment, stemming from an intention to treat someone less favourably on prohibited grounds, and disparate impact, as in the *Griggs* case. It inspired the distinction in British law between direct discrimination (corresponding to disparate treatment) and indirect discrimination, which occurs when someone imposes a condition which has a disparate and unfavourable impact on a racial or gender group and which cannot be shown to be justifiable on other grounds (what in the US would be 'business necessity'). In both the US and Britain the employer has to justify to the court any practice which occasions disparate impact.

As an example of a failed allegation of disparate treatment, it is interesting to consider the case of *Sirajullah v. Illinois State Medical Inter-Ins. Exch*. Sirajullah was a surgeon who had sought insurance against claims from patients alleging malpractice on his part. The company refused to insure him because his 'foreign accent' would, allegedly, have made it more difficult for him to communicate with patients, and thus more susceptible to malpractice claims. In Britain there have been cases in which the denial of service to a telephone enquirer speaking with a foreign accent has been considered evidence of discrimination. The reaction to the accent has been regarded as evidence of action on grounds of that person's race. The legal position is similar in the US. In both countries an employer may treat people differently on the basis of their job ability. The court in Sirajullah's case took note that the defendants had rejected 19 other applicants on the same grounds and therefore concluded that he had not been treated differently from similarly-situated applicants. A British court might well have wanted evidence to support the assumption that a strange accent would lead to more malpractice claims.

In the US law books disparate treatment is illustrated by cases such as *McDonnell Douglas Company v. Green*, in which a black employee who had been laid off joined with others in obstructing traffic into the plant and was convicted for an offence against the criminal law. Later the employer re-engaged the whites involved, but not the black man. The court held that discrimination could be inferred in such circumstances unless the employing company could articulate some legitimate reason for its action. US courts have extensive powers to order remedial action. Thus in *United States v. Philadelphia*, in 1978, the police department was ordered to make up for past discrimination by hiring 20 female out of 120 new officers; to facilitate the transfer of female officers, and to reinstate a recruit whose training had been terminated because of pregnancy. When employers have introduced hiring policies which favour disadvantaged groups they have sometimes had to defend themselves against suits brought by white males who might have been hired but for these policies. They can claim that they have been treated less favourably on the grounds of their race or ethnic origin or gender, and that they are therefore the victims of 'reverse discrimination'. The most celebrated of these cases was that of *Regents of the University of California v. Bakke* in 1978, which divided the Supreme Court and demonstrated that when quotas are used as a means of remedy so many variables can be taken into account that there can be no simple and clear-cut legal solution.

The relation between direct and indirect discrimination in British law is illustrated by the case of *Hurley v. Mustoe*, in which a woman was refused employment as a waitress in a small restaurant on the grounds that it was not the employer's policy to employ women with small children because in his experience they were unreliable as workers. An Industrial Tribunal dismissed the complaint as, in their view, it was not the employer's policy to employ anyone, man or woman, who had small children. On appeal, it was found that no evidence had been adduced to show that it was not the employer's policy to employ men with small children; since there was no evidence that men with small children were unreliable it-had not been demonstrated that the policy was necessary for the running of such a business and therefore justifiable in law. Some women with small children might be unreliable, but the employer had not enquired about Mrs Hurley's arrangements for the care of her children should they fall sick. Nor had he enquired of her previous employers about her reliability. He had treated her differently on the grounds of her sex and therefore had discriminated directly.

In considering whether discrimination has occurred in an inter-view for a job, a tribunal will be interested to hear what questions were asked of an applicant. If, for example, questions concerning responsibility for children were asked of a female applicant but not of male applicants, this will be taken as evidence that women were being treated less favourably. Questions have to be job-related, and the law assumes that both fathers and mothers are responsible for the care of their children.

The case of *James v. Eastleigh Borough Council* arose because Mr James had to pay to use the swimming pool and his wife did not. They were both aged 63. The Council's policy was to allow free entry to people of pensionable age, which the state had fixed at 60 for women and 65 for men. Was the Council discriminating on grounds of sex? The first court decided that they were not. On appeal this view was confirmed, but it was held that reliance on the state rule might be indirectly discriminatory and that therefore the case should be reheard on a different basis. On further appeal, the House of Lords concluded that the state rule was inherently discriminatory and that in relying upon it the Council had discrimi-nated directly. This case confirmed the view that the test to apply is to ask 'would the applicant have been treated differently *but for* his or her sex?'. This same test will be used in cases of racial discrimination.

A court has sometimes to decide whether an applicant belongs to a protected class. Two cases were decided by the US Supreme Court in 1987 which illustrate this. In one, the Shaare Tefila Congregation instituted a civil rights action against eight men accused of defacing

their synagogue with antisemitic slogans. The first court dismissed
their suit, holding that discrimination against Jews is not racial
discrimination, and this view was upheld on appeal. In the other
case Saint Francis College defended itself against a suit brought by a
professor who claimed that he had been denied tenure because of
his Arab origin and Muslim religion. The first court held that the law
did not cover claims of discrimination based an ancestry, but this
was reversed on appeal. The Supreme Court heard the two final
appeals on the same day. Counsel for the Congregation did not
argue that the Jews were a separate race, but that the animus against
them had been racial; since whites who had been victimized by
other whites for giving support to the rights of blacks had been given
the Court's protection, so should her clients. This raised the
question of whether an alleged discriminator was mistaken in
identifying the victim racially. Seeking criteria as to who was
protected by race, the justices asked about the relation of race to
national origin, colour, ethnicity, physiognomy, ancestry and stock.
A unanimous Supreme Court later held that for a charge of racial
discrimination to be made out it was necessary to demonstrate not
only that the defendants were motivated by racial animus but that
the animus was directed towards the kind of group that Congress
intended to protect in 1866 when it passed the statute. Jews and
Arabs could bring suit because they were among the peoples
considered to be distinct races when the statute was enacted,
whether or not these groups could be considered racial in modern
scientific theory. A distinctive physiognomy was not essential to
qualify for protection. Discrimination based upon ancestry or
ethnic characteristics could be discrimination in law.

A comparable case in Britain arose when a Mr Mandla sought a
place in a private school for his son. Mr Mandla was a Sikh who
insisted that his son must wear a turban. The school was multi-racial
and there were Sikh pupils who did not wear turbans. The head-
master denied Mr Mandla a place because turban-wearing was
contrary to the school's rules about the way pupils should be
dressed. He could not approve of an exception to them which would
draw attention to differences between pupils. Was this racial
discrimination? The first court held that the Sikhs were a religious
and not a racial group, so the suit was dismissed. This decision was
upheld in the Court of Appeal but reversed in the House of Lords
which held that for a group to constitute an ethnic group in law it
must regard itself, and be regarded by others, as a distinct

community by virtue of certain characteristics. Two characteristics were essential. First, a long shared history, of which the group was conscious as distinguishing it from other groups, and the memory of which it kept alive; and second, a cultural tradition of its own, including family and social customs and manners, often but not necessarily associated with religious observance. Other relevant, but not essential, characteristics were a common geographical origin, or descent from a small number of common ancestors, and a common language, literature or religion. This decision clarifies the position as to who may claim protection under the prohibition of indirect discrimination but does not bear upon the grounds of the discriminator's action. There are Sikhs and Jews who do not practice the religion of their group. If they claim that they have been subjected to less favourable treatment, under English law they have to prove that this was on the grounds of their ethnic origins, because there is no prohibition upon discrimination on grounds of religion. The Mandla case established that Sikhs were entitled to try and do this.

There is an important tension between the legal tests for deciding whether something is contrary to the prohibition of actions which are discriminatory in purpose and those which are discriminatory in effect. If the English 'but for' test be employed, a court has to decide whether someone would have been treated differently *but for* his or her race or sex. When the allegation is of discriminatory purpose, this becomes a subjective test. Would Jones have treated Smith more favourably but for his belief that Smith was a Jew? The court has to examine the evidence about the attitudes and state of mind of Jones. Is it clear that he believed the other man to be Jewish? And that his action was a consequence of this belief? Whether Smith was or was not a Jew is irrelevant. When the allegation is of discriminatory effect, it is the other way round. Smith can claim the court's protection only if he can establish that he is a member of a protected class (as Mr Mandla had to). The test is objective. Was Smith a Jew? Was a condition imposed which was more difficult for Jews to meet, which could not be justified on non-discriminatory grounds and was unfavourable? Jones' intention is irrelevant. One day a court may have to consider a case in which these two approaches are in conflict with one another.

In Britain no court has any power to impose recruitment quotas, though the Commission for Racial Equality, if it has established that some employer or local authority is practising racial discrimination, and if it has issued a non-discrimination notice, can then go to court to have it enforced. The other party may have to undertake remedial measures if it is to satisfy the court that it is complying with the order. In Britain it is unlawful to show preference to members of a racial group in order to compensate for past discrimination. Nor may a class action be brought on behalf of a class of alleged victims; the action has to be in the name of an individual or individuals, and, if it succeeds, others may benefit from the principle that has been established.

In Germany, however, some of the *länder* (or provinces) have introduced legally-binding quota systems for women in public employment (in local government, schools and universities). How these systems will develop is still uncertain.

Other grounds of discrimination

The Americans With Disabilities Act, which entered into force in 1992, has been described as the most sweeping civil rights legislation since the Civil Rights Act of 1964. It protects some 43 million people, of whom about 44 per cent have physical disabilities, 32 per cent health impairments, 13 per cent visual, hearing and speech impediments, and 6 per cent mental disabilities; they are a far from homogeneous category of people. The Act declares that no institution covered by law (what is inelegantly referred to as a 'covered entity'),

> shall discriminate against a qualified individual in regard to job application procedures, the hiring, advancement, or discharge of employees, employee compensation, job training, and other terms, conditions, and privileges of employment.

Apart from employment, it covers public services, including transport, public accommodation, and telecommunications. Its introduction means that restaurants, hotels, stores and theatres can no longer turn away a person with cerebral palsy, epilepsy, AIDS, or any other disability. Employers must take reasonable steps to make workplaces accessible to the disabled. Stores have to re-arrange merchandise, car rental agencies have to make available some cars with hand controls, telephone companies must be able to pass on messages from persons who use special keyboard phones, and more buses have to be equipped with lifts to take wheelchairs – as in Germany.

In order to achieve worthy aims the law requires employers to follow procedures that can in some special circumstances have strange results. There may be no health check on a potential employee until after a decision has been reached to offer that person a job. Thus if a blind person applies to become a police officer and attends for interview carrying a white stick and assisted by a guide dog, the interviewer can ask only if the applicant can obtain a licence to drive a car, and cannot ask why not. The job decision has to be taken first.

The EU has issued a recommendation to member states advising them to 'provide fair opportunities for disabled people in the field of employment and vocational training' but this does not have the legally binding effect of a directive.

In the United Kingdom the Disabled Persons (Employment) Act of 1944 imposed upon employers of more than 20 employees a duty to fill at least 3 per cent of jobs with registered people. Many employers fail to meet their quota and have to seek exemption, which is more easily obtained than in Germany where fines are imposed on organizations which fail to meet their quotas, the money being used to finance training for people with disabilities. The Companies Act (1985) requires companies employing more than 250 workers to include in their annual reports a statement about what they have been doing to improve opportunities for disabled people, and a Code of Good Practice on the Employment of Disabled People has been issued. Parliament has more recently considered proposals to prohibit discrimination on grounds of disability but the bill is unlikely to become law. The government has also ruled out any prospect of legislating against discrimination on grounds of age. Many would argue that any unequal treatment of persons as a result of disability or age can be rectified better by non-legal measures.

For example, in Britain, as in many other countries – though not the USA, bank notes of different value are of different size. One reason for this is to make it easier for blind or partially sighted people to recognize the value of a note they are giving or receiving. Were the law to outlaw indirect discrimination on grounds of disability, the Bank of England might be acting unlawfully if it reduced the difference in size between notes of different denomination, but the same results can be attained by private negotiation. Successful representations have also been made about modifying polling stations to make it easier for blind and partially-sighted people to vote, but attempts to have the needs of such people mentioned in the British government's Jobseeker's Charter came to little.

Discrimination on grounds of religion is prohibited in a number of countries, including Canada, New Zealand and the USA. All countries require lawful discrimination on grounds of age when they stipulate that persons of less than a certain age may not marry, smoke, drink intoxicating liquor, drive motor cars, and so on. A few, including Canada and the USA, have legislated to prohibit the refusal of employment to people on the grounds of their being too old when the job applicants have not been tested to see whether they are capable of doing the work. The government of the UK has refused to support such proposals.

In 1984 the European Parliament deplored 'all forms of discrimination based upon an individual's sexual tendencies' and called upon member states and the EU Commission to act against such discrimination. Specific prohibitions have been enacted in France (against unequal treatment based on *moeurs* – or lifestyle), in Denmark on such treatment based on sexual orientation, in the Netherlands on 'heterosexual or homosexual orientation' and, within Germany, by the *Land* Brandenburg on sexual orientation. In Ireland it has been made a criminal offence to incite to hatred on the basis of sexual orientation. The unequal treatment of homosexuals raises some special issues which are best discussed in Chapter 6.

In the course of the Black Power movement of the late 1960s in the USA frequent reference was made to institutional discrimination as an attitude pervading a society which resulted in the subordination of a group. It could be used to denote any of the forms of discrimination discussed in this chapter. Yet while discriminatory practices are often taken for granted in many communities and organizations, and in this sense discriminatory behaviour is institutionalized, the expression 'institutional discrimination' itself is of doubtful value and lacks any legal foundation. To some extent it has been superceded by the development of the law against discrimination in effect. To reduce discrimination it is necessary to locate the actual points at which it occurs, using the methods described in Chapter 2, and then to hold particular individuals and organizations responsible for the practices that have been uncovered.

Conclusion

This chapter has provided a brief review of the development of international law against discrimination, both through the United Nations and the European Union. The task of enforcing that law falls to governments, which meet their obligations in different ways and in varying degrees. The extent of the protection envisaged has been greatly extended by acceptance of the principle that the law should prohibit action which is discriminatory in effect (what might be called unconscious discrimination) as well as that which is discriminatory in its purpose (or conscious discrimination). From the UN Charter's original intention to protect human rights 'without distinction as to race, sex, language or religion', the movement has spread in some countries to define as discriminatory the unequal treatment of disabled persons, the elderly and homosexuals. If the laws are to be effective in influencing the behaviour of millions of people, the courts will have increasingly to address certain problems in their application and the general public will need a better understanding of the reach of the law.

5

Remedies and their Effectiveness

If the best protections against discrimination are in people's hearts, then the best remedy for someone who has been the victim of discrimination is for the person responsible voluntarily to apologize, offer recompense, and change his or her practice. But often an allegation of discrimination will be contested, and perhaps for good reason. Laws are needed to strengthen protection and to provide for the adjudication of complaints. These laws often have an important educational value. Questions then arise as to the kinds of laws which are most effective.

ICERD Article 6 requires States Parties to 'assure to everyone in their jurisdiction effective protection and remedies'. CEDAW in Article 2 requires States Parties to 'ensure through competent national tribunals and other public institutions the effective protection of women against any act of discrimination'. Under EU law also, states are required to provide effective remedies. Unlike discrimination on grounds of sex, racial discrimination in certain settings has in some countries been made a criminal offence, but that does not mean that the criminal law necessarily or always offers the best way of counteracting it. In the German and Netherlands legal systems an incident in which a restauranteur, hotelier or dance hall proprietor has discriminated by failing to serve someone, may be best dealt with under administrative law. Anyone providing a service to the public needs a licence, and this can be withdrawn if that person has offended. If a government department has been interpreting its duties in a questionable manner, the best place to call it to account may be in a constitutional court. Elsewhere, and particularly in the Nordic countries, labour law has been developed to furnish remedies for discrimination, while in some countries there is an ombudsman with power to investigate such cases.

In Chapter 3 it was argued that an individual might discriminate because of pressures from others. Sometimes people are incited to discriminate racially by those who maintain that members of some minority have no right to be in the country. Propaganda of this kind is a threat to public order and is therefore to be dealt with by the criminal law in the same manner as comparable threats. So, too, are racial attacks and racial harassment.

One of the chief influences in the drafting of the racial convention was the belief that a major cause of racial discrimination was the dissemination of doctrines of racial superiority. States were therefore required by Article 4(b) to 'declare illegal and prohibit organizations . . . which promote and incite racial discrimination'. This sentence is preceded by one earlier in the same article which says that any measures shall be undertaken 'with due regard to the principles embodied in the Universal Declaration of Human Rights'. Nevertheless the peremptory language of Article 4(b) led several western states to enter reservations on this point when they ratified the Convention. Thus France stated that in its view the due regard clause released states 'from the obligation to enact anti-discrimination legislation which is incompatible with the freedoms of opinion and expression and of peaceful assembly and association'. Those freedoms are defined in Articles 19, 21 and 22 of the International Covenant on Civil and Political Rights. Most governments in North America and western Europe share the view that it is wrong to ban organizations for what their members say they believe. If they are to be banned, it should be for what they have done. If they threaten the public peace, then possibly they can be declared illegal under the criminal law, but experience in Northern Ireland does not demonstrate that much is gained by making the IRA (Irish Republican Army) an illegal organization. The wisdom of the British government in prohibiting direct reporting of the speeches of IRA representatives is widely questioned.

In the United States, law and opinion both support freedom of speech on political matters to an extent that a Nazi organization was allowed to march in a Chicago suburb whose residents included many survivors of the Holocaust. The American Civil Liberties Union (ACLU) maintains that the banning of racist speech may only aggravate racism (Colliver 1992: 319–22). The peoples' democracies of eastern Europe were very ready to prohibit racist organizations, but experience after 1989 did not suggest that they had been any more successful than western countries in eliminating the sentiments that such organizations exploit. It looks as if effective counteraction often depends upon the institutions that come between the state and the citizen: the neighbourhood, work and friendship groups, and the public services like the police.

Criminal and civil law

Criminal offences are offences against the state, and are to be distinguished from civil wrongs, which are disputes between citizens in which the state may have no interest. Because of this fundamental difference legal proceedings are also different. Civil proceedings may offer the victim of racial discrimination more effective remedies, because:

1 The standard of proof is different. In criminal proceedings the state, being so powerful, is required to prove its case beyond reasonable doubt. In civil proceedings, the plaintiff needs only to prove his or her case on the balance of probabilities.
2 In criminal proceedings the accused may have a right of silence, both in police custody and in court. He or she need not then testify and expose himself or herself to cross-examination, and no inference of guilt can be drawn from such silence. Under the Britsh law on racial discrimination, if the respondent does not reply the tribunal can infer that the applicant's statement of the facts is reliable.
3 It is usually the police who initiate criminal proceedings, though the prosecutor takes the final decision. Victims or their relatives sometimes complain about a reluctance to prosecute or to prefer the most serious charge. In racial discrimination cases the applicant has unhindered access to the tribunal.
4 Criminal proceedings have an all-or-nothing character (though the prosecutor sometimes accepts a guilty plea to a lesser charge instead of continuing with a contested hearing on a more serious charge). In racial discrimination cases the parties can settle privately without any admission of fault by the respondent.

This comparison can draw some support from the position in France where the primary remedies for all kinds of racial discrimination lie in the criminal law. By 1991 the annual number of convictions had risen to 101, almost entirely for offences against public order, namely for incitement to racial hatred, insult, defamation (often offences in the press) and for refusal to serve. There were just four convictions for racial discrimination in employment, which scarcely suggests that criminal remedies are effective in this field. (In 1990 in Germany there were 370 recorded cases of incitement to racial hatred and 111 convictions; there are still no effective protections against racial discrimination in employment.)

In Britain someone who suspects that he or she has received less favourable treatment on grounds of race or sex can go to the regional industrial tribunal office and fill out a form. He or she then becomes an applicant, while the person or company complained against becomes the respondent. A copy of the form is sent to the respondent who has to reply to the allegation. Copies of the form and of any reply go to the Advisory, Conciliation and Arbitration Service (ACAS) which writes to the parties, offering to help them to reach a settlement without the matter having to go before a tribunal.

By the end of the 1980s round about 1000 cases per annum of alleged racial discrimination and a slightly higher number of cases of alleged sex discrimination were being reported to industrial tribunals. Reports of racial discrimination were rising at nearly 25 per cent per annum, and of sex discrimination at over 60 per cent per annum. Nearly one in four of both kinds of case were being settled as a result of conciliation by ACAS. About 40 per cent of the race and 30 per cent of the sex cases were being adjudicated by tribunals. In about 8 per cent of the race and slightly more of the sex cases the tribunal was reaching a finding of discrimination; in most of the others it was dismissing the application, though some applications were found to lie outside the scope of the tribunal's powers or raised issues that were dealt with in some other way.

Of the cases left after allowing for conciliation, well over a third were being withdrawn by the applicant. Some would have been withdrawn because the parties had come to a private settlement: the applicant could have been assisted by a solicitor or a trade union official who negotiated a solution to the complaint and possibly a payment in compensation. In other cases the applicant, after receiving the respondent's reply, may have felt that the chances of a favourable outcome were too slender for it to be worth continuing, or have lost heart for some other reason and abandoned the application.

Some applications are dismissed when the proceedings fail to establish that it was on racial grounds that the applicant was denied a job, or was dismissed. The law recognizes that discrimination is difficult to prove, and tries to allow for this. Even when an application is dismissed, the proceedings may still serve to draw employers' attention to the law's requirements. A review of the decisions of the industrial tribunal in Bristol over the years 1980–89 inclusive (Banton 1990: 138) found four instances in which, though the application was dismissed, the tribunal commented adversely upon the failure of the employer to institute or implement an equal opportunities policy in conformity with the nationally approved Code of Practice. The respondents included departments of central and local government, a health authority and an aircraft manufacturer. To quote the tribunal:

> it is clear from the evidence of the respondents that very little has been done to implement the terms of that Code . . . the respondents had no written policy for tackling racial discrimination and no person had overall responsibility for the supervision of matters concerned with racial discrimination. We believe that this is lamentable in a company of this size.

And again:

> The statistics produced by the respondent were totally useless . . .

When a managing director receives a copy of a tribunal decision which includes severe criticism, the personnel manager's continued employment could well be called into question. A recent examination of 574 cases found that the managers involved experienced them as unpleasant. They thought they were on trial for failing to manage properly or for acting maliciously, and they resented the charges. Some found them humiliating. The research workers commented:

> The thing feared most . . . is the judgement that discrimination has occurred . . . passions were raised by the thought of being branded officially as a discriminator. For some, this was important for business, particularly for employers selling goods and services to the public sector; for others it was important personally.
>
> (McCrudden *et al*. 1991: 264–5)

Some applications are dismissed because the complaint is without foundation, or even mischievous. Among the Bristol cases were five applications in the same year from a doctor alleging discrimination in that he had not been called for interview after having applied for appointment as a Consultant Surgeon. On the first occasion he twice failed to attend the hearing. In later cases his complaint was struck out as frivolous and vexatious and he was ordered to pay costs to the respondents. Under Section 20 of the Employment Act 1989, the Secretary of State now has power to introduce a requirement that applicants put down a deposit of £150.

Since so many of the problems of racial discrimination are bound up with the problems of inner city neighbourhoods and public housing, it is relevant to note that civil remedies have advantages over criminal ones in this field. Following the example of the housing department in Chicago, the director of housing in Hackney, London, has obtained court injunctions against named trouble-makers on what are euphemistically known as 'difficult estates'. Because defendants may, after charge, be released on bail and then terrorize those who would testify against them, it can be difficult to secure criminal convictions. But the use of a civil injunction means that if defendants break it they can be immediately imprisoned, and, if they are tenants of public housing, they can lose their tenancies.

A comparison

One way of assessing the effectiveness of laws against discrimination is to compare them with the effectiveness of laws against crime. It is easier to do this for laws against racial than sex discrimination.

Several countries now undertake periodic surveys of their public which ascertain, among other things, what has been their experience of crime in the recent past. One such, the 1988 British Crime Survey (BCS) was based on interviews in which respondents were asked questions like 'In the last twelve months, has anyone got into your home without permission, in order to steal?' Those who said this had happened to them had not always reported the incidents to the police, often because the loss was trivial or the victim thought there was little chance of the offender being apprehended. Apart from the dark figure of unreported crime there is a grey figure of instances reported but not recorded by the police in the way the victim proposes. What the victim assumes to be burglary the police may consider to be theft or criminal damage. There are also false reports. For example, men who have lost their weekly wages gambling or on a visit to a prostitute, may invent a story of being robbed, and report it, so that they have an excuse when they get home without any money. Therefore, it is not surprising that when the BCS figures were compared with police records, it transpired that only 17 per cent of the survey incidents of robbery, and 41 per cent of those of burglary, had been recorded as such.

Though there is much under-recording of criminal offences, it seems (to judge from other research) to be less than the under-reporting of experiences of racial discrimination at work. Since racial discrimination will be experienced mostly by members of minority ethnic groups, these figures should be compared with their reporting of crime. In the BCS, the percentages of interviewees saying that they had been the victims of robbery (including theft from the person) varied from 1.1 for whites to 3.0 for Asians and 3.3 for Afro-Caribbeans. The percentages saying that they had been the victims of burglary varied from 5.6 for whites to 6.2 for Asians and 10.3 for Afro-Caribbeans. Much of the variation could be attributed to social and demographic factors (poor people more often suffer burglary and young males are more often attacked). It is also important to make allowance for the residential differences: a higher proportion of members of minority ethnic groups live in high-crime neighbourhoods. The BCS found that generally there was little difference in the level at which whites, Asians and Afro-Caribbeans reported offences to the police, so comparisons are not rendered unreliable on this account.

Table 2 brings together the figures that have been discussed above. The first column starts with an estimate of the number of cases in which persons are refused employment on grounds of race. Since there is no good estimate of the number of cases in which persons are refused employment on grounds of sex, it has not been possible to include a column for that. The actual numbers of crimes have been adjusted to the same base as that for column one. A fourth column giving the figures for notifiable crimes for 1990 has been added; when compared with BCS figures it shows the differences between the dark and grey figures of crime. If, in column one, allowance is made for the proportion of racial discrimination cases which are resolved by private settlement, and the resulting figure is compared with the proportion of criminal offences which result in conviction, it would seem that the success rates for all columns are not greatly different.

In British law it is now established that an employer has a duty to

Table 2   Cases of racial discrimination and crime compared

	Racial discrimination at work	Robbery	Burglary	Total crime
Cases	10 000	10 000	10 000	10 000
Reported	1 000	–	–	4 100
Recorded	–	7 629	5 085	2 600
Adjudicated	410	–	–	–
Proven	80	459	305	300
Success rate (per cent of cases)	3.5–5	4.6	3	3

Sources: Col 1, estimate from McCrudden *et al.* 1991: 123; cols 2 and 3, estimates from Home Office (1989) adjusted to similar baseline; crime figures from Home Office (1988); col 4 from Home Office (1991b).

Note: The fourth line down gives, in col 1, the number of applications upheld at industrial tribunals, and in the other columns, numbers of criminal convictions.

protect an employee from racial or sexual abuse. For example, the Metropolitan Police paid out £20,000 to a police constable with ethnic origins in West Africa who had been subjected to racial abuse from other police officers. Sexual harassment has been defined as including not only unwelcome acts which involve physical contact of a sexual nature, but also contact falling short of such acts and behaviour that is not intended to harass. This includes the making of suggestive remarks, telling offensive jokes, deliberately staring, or behaviour with sexual innuendo. This is in line with the European Commission's code which covers conduct that creates an intimidating, hostile or humiliating working environment. A man can claim sexual harassment if he is harassed by either a woman or another man, as can a woman who is harassed by a man or another woman.

The procedures established under the Sex Discrimination and Race Relations Acts are becoming increasingly effective. The number of persons making use of their remedies goes up year by year. A black man serving a prison sentence who was denied the opportunity to work in the prison kitchen when other prisoners whose records were no better than his were allowed to do so, succeeded in the case he brought against the government for discrimination. A civil court has overturned the decision of a military court which did not follow the proper procedures when dealing with a case which involved charges of racial discrimination. Proceedings have been brought against the police by serving police officers who have alleged racial and sex discrimination within the police.

In the United States someone who believes that he or she has suffered discrimination can usually take advantage of either a state or a federal remedy or both. Thus in Washington, DC, for example, such a person can go to the Department of Human Rights and Minority Business Development where a counsellor will help that person draw up a complaint in the proper form. A fact-finding conference is held involving the complainant and the respondent which will attempt to achieve an equitable settlement. The complaint may be dismissed or result in a finding of 'probable cause', which would lead to an attempt at conciliation. Failing this, the Commission on Human Rights may adjudicate, or the complainant may pursue the matter through the courts.

The effectiveness of such remedies may be judged by the proportion of aggrieved persons who achieve a result that is to their satisfaction, but some victims do not complain and some grievances are not justified. It is better to repeat a situation test (see Chapter 3: 28–34) after a lapse of years. One such repetition in Britain found no reduction in discrimination after nine years (Brown and Gay 1985). Any consideration of the effectiveness of the legislation itself has to take a wider view, starting from the overall situation which the legislation was intended to rectify. It was hoped that the US and British legislation would result in a more proportionate representation of minorities in the higher-status positions, the better-paid posts, the preferred residential neighbourhoods, and so on.

One justification for the imposition of job quotas in the US (mentioned on pp. 43 and 45) was the urgency of the need to overcome the effects of inherited disadvantage. Within the majority white populations of North American and west European societies, high levels of inter-generationally transmitted inequality seem to be tolerated because its incidence is less apparent when people are of the same colour and some of them are known to have climbed up or fallen down the social ladder by comparison with their parents. The inherited disadvantage of blacks is more obvious and, because people of distinctive colour are more easily stereotyped, this kind of transmitted inequality is more self-sustaining (see pp. 15–16). It is also the more dangerous socially and politically. Since laws which furnish remedies against discrimination to individuals have little effect upon inherited disadvantage, there may be a case for more drastic intervention, but any argument in favour of quotas quickly becomes a highly political issue and needs a book to itself.

Enforcement agencies

The opportunity for aggrieved individuals to apply for redress to special tribunals is of the greatest importance, but is of only limited value when so many individuals do not have the money or the skills needed to pursue their cases. So governments in several countries have established special enforcement agencies empowered to initiate legal action and to help individual litigants. The earliest and most notable of these has been the Equal Employment Opportunity Commission in Washington, which inspired the creation in Britain of the Commission for Racial Equality and the Equal Opportunities Commission, and in Belgium and the Netherlands of somewhat similar bodies. An agency may be empowered to pursue a policy of strategic enforcement, selecting particular companies or institutions for investigation and bringing legal proceedings if they fail to rectify any shortcomings that are discovered. The British Race Relations Act 1976 gave the Commission for Racial Equality important powers to conduct formal investigations, but Section 49(4) made the procedure so elaborate and cumbersome that a recalcitrant defendant can frustrate the whole process. This deficiency was made apparent by a court judgement in 1982 but successive governments have been unwilling to amend the section.

In the United States there are five major branches of the federal government which exercise powers of enforcement, while a variety of other federal bodies have lesser duties in this field. At the head of the list is the Department of Justice with its special Office for Civil Rights. Its responsibilities include the enforcement of statutes guaranteeing the rights to register and vote without discrimination or intimidation, and the rights to full and equal enjoyment of goods, services and public accommodation. From time to time it files charges alleging abuse of federal civil rights law when state remedies have proven ineffective. The Department of Education is responsible for preventing segregation and assuring equality of opportunity for both pupils and their teachers. The Equal Employment Opportunity Commission handles all complaints of employment discrimination and funds many state and local government agencies which investigate and process such cases. The Department of Housing and Urban Development is authorized to initiate its own investigations and complaints regarding discrimination in the sale, rental, advertising or financing of housing. The fifth federal institution with special duties is the Federal Reserve Board, which has to coordinate anti-discriminatory action regarding credit transactions, including the racial distribution of home mortgage lending activities at the neighbourhood level.

Many of these agencies have a large backlog of cases which they have been unable to process, so that complainants have applied to courts for orders requiring them to expedite action. Staff shortages have delayed all attempts to accelerate the work that has to be done. Because complainants have different kinds of remedy available, it is not easy to compile simple statistics of cases, but it can be said that over the period 1971–91 their number has multiplied by about 26 times. By the end of that period there were over 100 000 employment complaints per year and nearly 10 000 regarding fair housing. In nearly half of the employment complaints, the EEOC was able to achieve a resolution involving a monetary settlement or some other adjustment like reinstatement in a post. In over a quarter of complaints no cause was found for any further proceedings. Rather less than 10 000 complaints resulted in proceedings in the federal courts, most of them being brought by private parties rather than by the enforcement agency. One striking feature of the position in the United States is the availability of so many alternative kinds of remedy. Most of the proceedings are in the civil courts but in some circumstances the enforcement agency may be able to bring criminal proceedings as well.

An enforcement agency may (as in Britain and the Netherlands) be authorized to prepare codes of good practice advising employers what they should do to avoid or eliminate discrimination. These codes, which may require government approval before they become official, can be compared with Highway Codes. They are not themselves law, but they set out the standards by which people can be judged if ever they have to defend themselves in an action before a court. There are parallels in the United States. For example, the Federal Department of Housing and Urban Development has entered into Voluntary Affirmative Marketing

Agreements with realtors and builders through which they seek to regulate themselves with minimum federal supervision.

Experience in the United States suggests that employers begin to take voluntary action when they believe it to their advantage to do so. Governments can manipulate the costs and benefits of compliance or non-compliance with their policies. Compliance is likely to be greater when

- the standard is established by law;
- there is a vigorous enforcement programme;
- the results are objectively measurable;
- there is lively and organized public concern (cf. Coussey 1992: 46–47).

In no country are all these conditions satisfied.

The Commission for Racial Equality finds that their best strategy is to concentrate upon employers who are regarded as leaders in their fields, and on issues or practices about which the industry itself is concerned. When information about inequalities and associated advice is tendered to such firms in private, they are more willing to act on the basis of this and their practice may spread to other employers.

Equal opportunity policies

Many laws are phrased in general terms and cannot deal with all the detail that has to be specified if the law is to be implemented in complex institutions. Laws against discrimination also need the support that can come from policies implemented in the workplace. It is therefore desirable for a great variety of bodies, professional associations, state services, private companies, hospitals, schools, and so on to have their own equal opportunities policies.

The procedural rules necessary to ensure that policies are put into practice can, by their detail, diminish the effect that policy statements are designed to secure. Therefore, in drafting an equal opportunities policy for an institution it can be best to separate matters of principle from the detail of implementation. An institution can well adopt an equal opportunities code, containing a very few statements of principle set out in simple terms. It can state the principles of equal treatment which it will follow in its appointments and promotions, in its dealings with customers or members of the public, and declare that incidents of abuse or harassment will be dealt with by its own internal disciplinary procedures. Such a code needs first to be the subject of wide consultation in the form of a preliminary draft, revised in the light of comments, then formally adopted and widely publicized. Each article of the code requires its own implementation statement explaining how the principle will be put into practice. Since circumstances change, these implementation statements can be the responsibility of specialist departments, able to revise them when necessary.

If an equal opportunities policy is to be effective it will need to be monitored. For example, the organization can produce an annual table listing the number of employees in various categories listed according to sex, ethnic origin, disability and whatever other classes are to be highlighted. It will then be possible to compare the figures and see whether there is any progress towards any targets for the more equal representation of women or other groups.

One value of such an approach is that it can serve as a reminder that the improvement of representation may be held back by a shortage of applicants from particular classes. An organization may need to increase the supply of candidates by advertising its interest in securing particular kinds of application.

To guard against discrimination in the recruitment process, job applicants can be asked to send to the personnel department of a company a completed form indicating their sex, ethnic origins, disability, etc. This form will not be seen by the appointing committee. But after the appointments for the year have been made it will be possible to see if the percentage of successful candidates was lower in some categories than others, and then, if necessary, to look and see if there were differences in the qualifications of candidates which explained the outcome. Monitoring like this can be a very useful check, but its value depends upon the willingness of people to complete such forms. People supply information about their age and sex without hesitation, but not everyone is prepared to complete a form about ethnic origins. People entitled to be registered as disabled often do not wish to be so registered (a survey in Britain found that 77 per cent of blind and partially-sighted people were not registered as such); so many of those with disabilities will not fill a section of a form which enquires about disability, while in most settings it will not be feasible to ask people to state their sexual orientation.

An equal opportunities policy may require those responsible for filling job vacancies first to draw up a job specification, to keep a record of applicants and the grounds for selecting some rather than others, both for interviewing and for subsequent job offers. Quite apart from their value as an external control, such requirements serve as a reminder to those making decisions of points they must carefully consider.

Extending the public sphere

One of the reasons for resisting equal opportunities measures is that they entail challenges to traditional assumptions (for example, as to what is men's and what is women's work), and introduce external rules into what have previously been self-regulating processes. They extend the sphere of public control and diminish that of private arrangement. In this they are part of a long-term trend. In the early phases of industrialization an employer believed that a decision about who was to be employed was something for him alone; a job was his private gift. In the German language the word for employer means a giver of work. This view was soon challenged by a movement which shaped a consciousness of a common class position and inspired a mass of labour legislation making the employment relationship subject to state control. Recent decades have seen comparable changes in other fields, including greater use of the law to regulate relations between couples and between parents and children.

Many car drivers used to think that it was their own business, and no one else's, if they drove after drinking alcohol – provided that no one was injured or inconvenienced thereby. Now a conviction for drunk driving carries a much greater public stigma and there is a greater acceptance of the need for the public regulation of drinking by drivers. The boundary between public and private has been moved, and the law has served an educational function. A similar process is to be observed in the requirement that those who ride motorcycles must wear crash helmets. If there is an accident in which a motorcyclist is injured, the driver of the vehicle which caused the injury is not indifferent to the extent of the injury. That driver, as well as the hospital that treats the injured person, has an interest in anything that minimizes the injury.

Many tobacco smokers used to believe they had the right to light up anywhere unless there was a fire risk. Many manufacturers were not worried about polluting the environment. There used to be little controversy about the use of animals in laboratory experiments.

Such things are now regarded as matters of *public* concern and there are vigorous disputes about where the line between private and public is to be drawn. Is abortion a question for private decision? Should people be allowed to hunt foxes with a pack of hounds and a troop of riders on horseback? Is bull-fighting a permissible sport? Should individuals be permitted to read pornographic literature or watch pornographic films in private, or does this encourage more violence against women and children? Should those individuals who enjoy hurting other people or being hurt be allowed to engage in sado-masochistic activities in private? (The British courts have decided that such behaviour, even when quite voluntary, can merit several years of imprisonment.) There are some people who believe that men and women ought not to eat meat because this practice corrupts the proper relationship between humans and other animals. So the boundary between private behaviour and the sphere of the public interest is subject to both contention and change.

The argument in favour of legislation against discrimination shares common elements with these other examples of the trend and is countered by similar objections about the need to preserve individual liberties and spheres of privacy.

Sex discrimination legislation challenges the assumption that women are responsible for child care and that this is in the private realm. Especially since the 1960s there has been a new consciousness among women of their common membership in a class that shares common problems. It has given rise, among other things, to a demand for 'gender-neutral' language. Whether a designation like 'chairman' has a gender bias, or is like words such as 'dog', 'duck' and 'peacock' which are applied both to a species and to a gender, is not something which can be settled by reference to a dictionary. Nomenclature often has to change with popular consciousness, while changes in vocabulary sometimes accelerate changes in that consciousness. Minority groups, like new nations, have often wanted to be known by new names. Legislation against racial discrimination challenges the assumption that physical appearance is a reliable indicator of a person's individual qualities. It seeks not to change private feelings but to prevent unfairness in public relations. The law regulates public life, and those areas of private life that people choose to bring within its scope (as by accepting the socially-recognized obligations of marriage, parenthood, etc., and by entering into relations governed by contract, e.g., landlord-tenant, employer-employee). Educational measures can influence both the public and the private spheres. Law influences the public sphere directly and the private sphere indirectly.

The educational value of law

Table 2 (p. 61) offers a comparison of the effectiveness of legal remedies for those who consider themselves victims of racial discrimination at work and for those who report they have been victims of crime. It is a measure of effectiveness relative to the frequency of incidents that are the subject of complaint. Yet an even better protection would be one that created a state of affairs such that there were scarcely any complaints in the first place. As a comparison, consider the limited effectiveness of the criminal law in cases of domestic violence. Usually it is the woman who is attacked, and often the incident results in the police being called. If the offender is prosecuted and punished, the whole household may suffer. So women are often disinclined to testify against their partners; they hope (often too optimistically) that the experience of a threatened prosecution will have a cautionary effect. In these and other circumstances it is more important to reduce the occasions for complaint than to improve the effectiveness of the remedies, important as this is. Legal measures need to be complemented by educational ones, including the use of the mass media to influence public opinion.

An alternative measure of the success of anti-discrimination policies is provided by the evidence of research into popular attitudes. In Britain, the first Race Relations Act of 1965 prohibited racial discrimination in hotels, restaurants, theatres, dance halls, public transport, and places of public resort generally. Parliament and the white public were not then persuaded that there was so much racial discrimination in other spheres that the law needed to be of wider scope. Social research in 1966–67 demonstrated, however, that racial discrimination was more frequent and widespread than even members of the victim groups believed. The evidence so impressed press commentators and parliamentarians that the 1968 Act was passed, extending the law's protections to the spheres of employment, housing, education and advertising. Over the period 1964–81, according to Gallup Poll surveys, although white objections to immigration remained strong, the proportion of whites saying that they would accept blacks or Asians as neighbours, friends, jobmates, bosses and relatives in-law increased.

Since 1965 white racial attitudes have changed very greatly. In 1991 an opinion poll conducted for the Runnymede Trust enquired 'Some people say Britain is a racist society in which black and Asian people have fewer opportunities than white people; others say Britain is a non-racist society in which people have equal opportunities regardless of race or ethnic background. Do you think Britain is a very racist society, fairly racist, fairly non-racist or a completely non-racist society?' Sixty-seven per cent of whites considered it to some extent racist. This is a world away from the replies that would have been received 30 years earlier. It testifies to the influence of publicity about individual cases and the results of research, and reveals an increased ability on the part of whites to understand the victims' perceptions.

In the same survey interviewees were asked 'Do you think people of Asian and West Indian origin are treated the same as whites, or better than whites, or worse than whites, by each of these groups of people?' Among white people, 38 per cent said they thought they were treated worse by employers, 48 per cent by the police and 24 per cent by the courts (for further figures see Table 3). There are no surveys from earlier years that would permit a close comparison, but those acquainted with white opinion would probably agree that these findings are further evidence of substantial attitude change. The eighth British Social Attitudes survey (Jowell and Airey 1991), asked interviewees to think of circumstances in which two people are charged with an offence, both being not guilty. Which would be the more likely to be declared guilty? Comparing for race, 3 per cent said the white person would be more likely to be convicted, 49 per cent said the chances were equal and 42 per cent that the black person was more likely to be convicted. This is a measure of public images, not of the reality. It conflicts with the findings of research summarized in Chapter 3 and would be contested by the police and by those responsible for court proceedings; they respond to the thought of being branded officially as discriminators as passionately as the employers mentioned on page 58. The figures can be compared with the 2 per cent who said that a rich man would be more likely to be convicted, the 38 per cent who said that rich and poor would have equal chances, and the 56 per cent who said that the poor person would be more likely to be convicted (Jowell *et al.*

Table 3 Expectations of discrimination

	Interviewees		
	White	Asian	Black
By employers	38	42	67
By police	48	44	75
By courts	24	19	57
By schools	13	15	38

Source: The Runnymede Trust, Race Issues Opinion Survey 1991, preliminary findings.

1991: 189–90). These figures suggest that the image is not one of race alone, but of race mixed with wealth.

In Britain, western Europe and North America over the past generation the movement against racial and sex discrimination has recorded both successes and disappointments. Expectations of greater equality have risen, while economic recession and the growth in the number of asylum-seekers has made its attainment the more difficult. Those who are impatient with the slow speed of change can take some comfort from the rapidity with which, since World War II, the realization has grown that no country can shut itself off from world events. What is happening on the other side of the world may soon affect the people of Europe. The mass media and the schools have taught these lessons to new generations so that now there is less racial prejudice among the young than the elderly, and less among the better educated.

Conclusion

Laws against discrimination play an essential part in the protection of rights, but they are not sufficient. Laws cannot regulate everything, and if they are to be effective they have to be supported by public sentiment. It is not to be expected that everyone will endorse such laws completely, especially when they run counter to other interests. Men may be less committed to equal opportunities than women, because their interests are different. Those who campaign for new laws are therefore well-advised if they campaign on a broad front, arguing that members of all the classes to be protected share a common interest in better protections, and that those who feel that their interests are threatened have an interest in seeing that any laws are drafted in a manner that is fair to them. As was pointed out in Chapter 2, men have an economic interest in the recognition of women's rights. For if the talents of women are better utilized, the national income increases, and, since men and women so often live together, all members of their households benefit from this increase. Legislation against discrimination is a response to 'market failure' in this respect.

The campaign for greater equality of opportunity is a continuing struggle, and perhaps it is as well that it should be since the struggle helps sustain the commitment to greater equality. This is the more important because of the limitations of state action. The objective of an equal opportunities campaign should be to see that all institutions, like professional associations, employers, state services, schools, hospitals, and so on, have their own policies which apply the general principles to the special features of their organizations and the way in which they operate.

6

Equal Treatment

Human rights are said to be universal. It is therefore unfair if the rights of people living in one state are better protected than those of people living in another. It is also inevitable that this will be the case. The state is the most effective institution for the protection of rights even if it is not the only one. Citizens have to co-operate in seeing that their legislatures enact appropriate laws and then enforce them. If they succeed, their actions benefit the generations to come. Those who press for better laws can appeal to shared religious beliefs and to international legal standards, but legal systems differ from one country to another so that laws have to be adapted to the different traditions.

Equal or equivalent?

The principle of equal treatment is recognized in Article 1 of the constitution of the Netherlands, which declares that 'persons shall be treated equally in equal circumstances'. The principle holds that like things, or people, should be treated alike, and unlike things, or people, treated differently. Discrimination is wrong because it breaches this principle. However, as this chapter will go on to discuss, there is no equally clear way of determining what things, or people, are alike. Before doing so, it is best to make clear that equal treatment is the objective, education and law being means of attaining that objective. Education entails more than schooling; it comprehends all the intellectual and moral influences on a child's upbringing. While law mostly works in a negative way, by imposing sanctions for deviance, it also has important educational value. As a means of combating discrimination, law works through the creation of protected classes; this may result in only rough justice, since not all members of a class are equally placed. One of the main criticisms of affirmative action in the United States has been that it has primarily benefited middle-class women and blacks, people who were well able to look after their own interests and less deserving of assistance than those trapped in the under-class. The creation of privileged classes benefiting from quota hiring has been intended to secure equal treatment for individuals in the long run, but as it is never possible to define these classes so exactly that only the most deserving benefit, the short-run results may be open to criticism.

What people are alike? Those who subscribe to a particular religious faith may believe that God created the world in accordance with a plan such that men and women, or people of different races, occupy different places in the scheme of creation. They are therefore different, and are not to be treated alike. This problem takes specific forms in some of the reservations made by states when acceding to the Convention on the Elimination of Discrimination against Women and the Convention on the Rights of the Child.

For example, Article 16 of the Convention on the Elimination of All Forms of Discrimination against Women begins: 'States Parties shall take all appropriate measures to eliminate discrimination against women in all matters relating to marriage and family relations and in particular shall ensure, on a basis of equality between men and women . . .', continuing in section (c) 'The same rights and responsibilities during marriage and at its dissolution'. Upon ratification of its accession to this treaty the government of Egypt made a reservation with respect to Article 16 stating that its accession was

> without prejudice to the Islamic Shariah's provisions whereby women are accorded rights equivalent to those of their spouses so as to ensure a just balance between them. This is out of respect for the sacrosanct nature of the firm religious beliefs which govern marital relations in Egypt and which may not be called in question and in view of the fact that one of the most important bases of these relations is an equivalency of rights and duties so as to ensure complementarity which guarantees true equality between the spouses. The provisions of the Shariah lay down that the husband shall pay bridal money to the wife and maintain her fully and shall also make a payment to her upon divorce, whereas the wife retains

full rights over her property and is not obliged to spend anything on her keep. The Shariah therefore restricts the wife's rights to divorce by making it contingent on a judge's ruling, whereas no such restriction is laid down in the case of the husband.

Objections to this reservation have been lodged by Germany, Mexico and Sweden which describe it as incompatible with the spirit and purpose of the Convention. These three states have objected, on the same grounds, to a variety of reservations regarding this and other articles of the Convention which have been made by Bangladesh, Brazil, Cyprus, Iraq, Jamaica, Korea, Mauritius, Thailand, Tunisia, and Turkey. There is a proposal that when questions are raised about the compatibility of a reservation with the spirit and purpose of a convention, an advisory opinion should be sought from the International Court of Justice.

Egypt entered no reservation with regard to the effect of CEDAW's Article 11, concerning the elimination of discrimination against women in the field of employment. New Zealand, however, reserved the right not to apply the Article 11 provision regarding the introduction of maternity leave with pay insofar as it was 'inconsistent with the policies relating to recruitment into or service in the Armed Forces which reflect . . . [service in] situations involving armed combat'. It also reserved the right not to apply anything inconsistent with the provisions of the ILO Convention concerning the Employment of Women on Underground Work in Mines of all Kinds, which New Zealand had ratified in 1938.

Thus Egypt's position is that women and men are alike in respect of their rights to work, but not in respect of divorce. New Zealand says that they are alike in respect of rights relating to marriage and family relations, but not with respect to all the various rights to equal treatment in the field of employment.

It is doubtful if a proper distinction can be drawn between equality and equivalence in the way the Egyptian reservation seems to imply. The idea of equality has its origins in a mathematical relation; equivalence can be no different. The Egyptian position appears to be that women are not equal to men in either the right to divorce or the right to maintenance. The wife's lesser rights in respect of divorce are balanced by her greater rights in respect of maintenance; add together the pluses and minuses and the total marital rights of the woman are equal to the total marital rights of the man. When seeking the proper comparator, it is necessary to study the total situation. The argument can continue by contending that it is more important to aim at equality between men and women over their whole life-span than at any particular point in it. The high level of divorce in western countries, coupled with the tendency for the bonds between mothers and children to be stronger than those between fathers and children, means that women there are often left at a disadvantage compared with men. Their equal rights to divorce provide only partial protection. For countries with other norms of marriage the best path may not lie in moving close to the western pattern.

Acceptance of the principle that men and women are equally responsible for child care cannot solve all the problems relating to discrimination on grounds of sex so long as it is women who give birth to babies. If a woman takes three months maternity leave, her position can be compared with that of a man who needs three months leave for medical treatment, but the man's leave does not result in the birth of a child whose rights may also demand consideration.

A case which throws into relief some of these difficulties was heard by the United States Supreme Court in 1991 (111 S Ct 1196). It was brought by a trade union against Johnson Controls, a company which used lead in the manufacture of batteries. The exposure of pregnant women to lead can result in miscarriages, premature delivery, stillbirths, low birth weight, developmental problems and the dysfunction of the central nervous system. The company had invested in lead-reduction technology and had warned women employees of the dangers, but some of them had given birth with excessive lead levels. So from 1982 it followed the practice of some other companies in prohibiting the employment of women in high-exposure posts. Other women employees were not affected by this.

Was the company's prohibition, in the terms of Title VII of the Civil Rights Act 1964, a practice which deprived a woman of an employment opportunity because of her sex? The first court decided that the company's policy was ostensibly neutral as between males and females but had a disparate impact upon females. Was this disparate impact justifiable? A majority of judges concluded that it was, but on appeal all the Supreme Court justices concurred in reversing that decision. One of them stated:

It is no more appropriate for the courts than it is for individual employers to decide whether a woman's reproductive role is more important to herself and her family than her economic role. Congress has left this choice to the woman as hers to make.

Women have a right equal with men to freedom of choice in employment. The misfortune of the company is that Title VII bars employers from considering the additional costs involved in employing female workers. If women ran the risks of exposure to lead, they and their children might subsequently sue the company on account of the injury they had suffered.

Does this decision protect the right of the child to health? Does the law ensure that the best interests of the child shall be a primary consideration for the state (in accordance with Article 3 of the Convention on the Rights of the Child)? The United States has not yet ratified this convention, but the question nevertheless deserves attention. There is a potential conflict between the right of the child and the right of the fertile woman without any corresponding conflict between the right of the child and the right of the fertile man, but the law can offer solutions only to legal problems.

Protected classes

Prohibitions of discrimination on grounds of race, sex, language and religion share common features, but they have all to be assessed against the objective of equal treatment. As a result there are differences between the various protected classes. In Britain the Sex Discrimination Act 1975 (sec. 49: 2) provides that a trade union may reserve seats on its governing body for persons of one sex when such persons would otherwise be under-represented. There is no corresponding provision in the Race Relations Act 1976 to permit a trade union to reserve seats on its governing body for members of minority ethnic groups. This was probably not an oversight. The distinction between males and females in the human species is relatively clear; it changes very little with the passage of centuries. Neither of these statements applies to distinctions of racial and ethnic origin. The International Convention on the Elimination of All Forms of Racial Discrimination presumes that racial discrimination *can* be eliminated, and the British government might say that the Race Relations Act was drawn up to eliminate and not perpetuate racial distinctions. To reserve seats for an indefinite period of time for members of a class defined by race or colour is to give those people an interest in maintaining their privilege and this will work to reinforce a distinction that the law seeks to eliminate. The same argument applies to the campaign in Britain for the creation of a separate black section within the Labour Party, paralleling the reservation of seats for women on its executive.

So if a British trade union decides (as the National Association of Teachers in Further and Higher Education did in 1991), to reserve three places on its national executive committee for blacks, it has to be careful. The trade union in question has an executive committee made up primarily of representatives of various constituencies; black members have been made into another constituency. Anyone wishing to be a candidate for one of the new seats has to state that he or she is a black member. All members of the union vote to elect all members of the executive committee irrespective of their constituencies.

The special class of members that has been created is one defined by colour and therefore it shares common features with any similar class defined by disability or age. Differences of colour, disability and age are continuous where differences of sex are discontinuous. There is a gradient of small colour differences from very light to very dark so that any colour categories depend upon arbitrary judgement. The same can be said of disability: disabled people have varying degrees of handicap. So classification by colour and disability can be practiced – as in the case of the trade union – only if it is is based upon self-assignment. If some individuals are accounted white and others non-white, there must be people who are on the borderline. Anyone investigating equality of treatment may find it necessary to ask them how, for any given purpose, they classify themselves. Equally there are people with disabilities who do not wish to draw attention to these and choose not to register themselves as disabled. However, it is not purely a matter of self-assignment to social categories. Someone could assign himself or herself to one colour category but be treated by others as if belonging in a different one. Someone who is not registered as disabled could still be regarded and treated as such.

This also has a bearing on the idea of equality. The goals of racial and sexual equality do not require that there should be equal numbers of persons of the different classes in all positions in society. Equality in the sense of equal treatment is the equal treatment of persons without regard to their membership in irrelevant social categories. Some individuals will deserve higher rewards because they make more valuable contributions; since groups differ in their cultures there will be some that invest more in their children's upbringing so that these in turn command a higher price for their labour. These groups will have higher average incomes. So long as there is a transmission of inequality from one generation to the next, the equal treatment of individuals can coexist with the inequality of groups. Transmitted inequality becomes the more important when it is associated with segregation. In many societies there is significant residential segregation associated with differences of socio-economic status and race; young people growing up in low-status neighbourhoods are likely to be at a disadvantage stemming from a variety of causes. There is considerable discrimination on grounds of social status and this becomes the more serious when it is compounded with racial differences.

The principle of equal treatment is the equal treatment of individuals, but humans cannot live just as individuals. They can survive physically and emotionally only as members of co-operating groups. Only some persons qualify to be members of groups, and members who do not observe the rules of groups have ultimately to be expelled. They have to be treated differently because they have become different. Decisions to admit some people rather than others to membership, and decisions to expel some persons, have to be based on the merits of the individuals in the light of rules of group membership that can be defended as fair and reasonable.

The family is a co-operating group which usually spans the generations and is a major transmitter of inequality. This should be recalled in connection with the prohibition in the International Bill of Human Rights upon distinctions of 'property, birth or other status'. Because of transmitted inequality, some individuals will enjoy advantages over others (most obviously in spending power). The prohibition states that such distinctions are irrelevant to peoples' entitlement to human rights.

Sociologists distinguish between a group and a category. A group is a class of persons who are conscious of belonging with one another and who recognize obligations of some sort towards fellow members. A category is a class whose nature and composition is decided by the definer; for example, persons earning wages in a certain range may be counted as a category for income tax purposes; persons aged between 35 and 39 are a category but not a group. Writers do not always observe this distinction, but it is important in connection with attitudes to racial and ethnic differences. The idea that human characteristics are the manifestations of a limited number of racial types led to a mode of classification that was thought to be objective; people were thought to belong in these categories whether or not they were conscious of it. The conception of human variation underlying this view was found to be mistaken, but not before some people had come to feel that they belonged to racial groups; in their case, categories had become groups.

National groups have often been regarded, and have regarded themselves, as biological in character when really they were social, political and cultural. So, since the 1930s, it has become conventional to call such groups ethnic and to say that they are defined by the shared ethnic origins of their members. They are true groups, whereas those which are called racial groups may be only categories. With respect to the prohibition of discrimination, the word 'racial' is more accurately applied to the attitude of the discriminator who treats people differently because he or she believes they belong in a racial category which it is appropriate to treat in a particular way. People are often assigned involuntarily to a racial category. The word 'ethnic' is more accurately applied to the group that results because people voluntarily identify themselves with others on the basis of a presumed common ethnic origin. Since there is often some admixture in people's ethnic origins, an individual often has a choice as to his or her ethnic identification and when a census is held, or enquiries are undertaken into ethnic discrimination, it is best if individuals are invited to assign themselves to an ethnic category. This is not to say that ethnicity is purely a subjective matter. It may be no use an individual counting himself or herself a member of a group if he or she is not accepted as a fellow-member by others. Therefore race and ethnic and national origin cannot be the bases for protected classes possessing the same clarity of definition as sex. They are more subject to manipulation and do not have such clear boundaries. While it is difficult for a person to belong to more than one sex class, assignment by race and ethnic and national origin is more flexible.

To be a member of a group based upon religion requires conscious identification by the person concerned, but protection is only called for when others behave less favourably towards that person because he or she is so identified. It seems to be less problematic than the other cases.

So far there has been little discussion of the nature of protected classes founded upon descent, political opinion, language and religion. The definition of racial discrimination in ICERD as including distinctions based upon descent covers some of the conflicts based upon clans or clan-like groupings that have occurred in Africa. It might also cover Hindu castes or *jatis*; the Indian government has denied that it does, but is an interested party in any debate on that matter. The prohibition of discrimination based upon political opinion is particularly apposite in circumstances where there is a national minority distinct from other citizens of the state. National minorities are often accused by governments of insufficient loyalty and may be the object of repressive measures. Often these minorities are marked by clear territorial, linguistic and cultural boundaries. Equal treatment with respect to language is not straightforward. In some countries members of linguistic minorities are not permitted to speak their mother-tongue in school. Sometimes parents want their children to receive their primary education in their mother-tongue and their secondary education in the national language. When pursuing a higher education in scientific subjects they may find it more acceptable to study in the national language than when specializing in the history or literature of the national minority. When the minority is small it may be expensive to provide public services or a television channel in the minority language. So if there is to be a protected class based upon language the extent of the protection has to be spelled out precisely.

Protected fields

A special kind of protected class has been created by the laws which, in order to facilitate the rehabilitation of offenders, allow for criminal convictions to be removed from a person's record. In Britain once a person's conviction is 'spent', that person may in certain circumstances lawfully deny that he or she has a criminal record in this respect. There are important exceptions dictated by the need to protect other persons. Thus sentences to serve a term of imprisonment exceeding thirty months are excluded from the provisions of the Rehabilitation of Offenders Act. Someone applying for a position of trust must reveal a conviction for dishonesty so that his or her suitability can be checked. Someone convicted for the abuse of a child may equally be thought unsuitable for appointment as a child care worker. So all convictions must be revealed by applicants for certain professions (medicine, law, accountancy, pharmacy), the armed services, police, prison or probation officer, care worker, firearms dealer, stockbroker, insurance manager, etc. These are fields explicitly excluded from the scope of protections extended to offenders.

The definition of the protected class and of protected fields can be more problematic when it comes to the prohibition of discrimination on grounds of sexual orientation. The boundaries to the protected class are not visible ones, as they are with race and sex, or as easily established as in the case of age and religion, but depend more upon self-assignment. Nor are they as stable, though some individuals have been homosexual all their adult lives and could not live in any other way. Many individuals are bisexual and can choose to behave in more than one way, so in this respect there is a continuum of degrees of homosexuality. Some people are heterosexual in one phase of their lives and homosexual in another phase. Some people have a homosexual identity, others a homosexual preference, and yet others engage in homosexual behaviour only occasionally. Both homosexuals and bisexuals at times behave in ways that do not distinguish them from heterosexuals and if they then receive equal treatment they require no special protection in these fields.

The question of protection arises when someone discriminates against a homosexual person because he or she is thought to be homosexual. This is to treat that person differently not because of anything that he or she has done, but because of the person's presumed membership in a class. Senior officers in the armed forces often believe that any personal obligations between members of their forces which can affect the manner in which they carry out their duties are contrary to good order and discipline. Sexual relations (whether heterosexual or homosexual) between two persons serving in the same unit can interfere with the chain of command and create suspicions of unequal treatment; their prohibition can therefore be justified. Sexual relations between a member of the armed forces and a non-member cannot have the same consequences. For a soldier to be dismissed from the army because he has had same-sex relations with a civilian (as happens) can only be justified if this fact constitutes grounds for apprehending a serious risk that he will engage in relations subversive of discipline.

All persons have a moral (and sometimes a legal) right to be protected from less favourable treatment occasioned by beliefs about what sorts of people they are rather than what they have actually done. One sequence of decisions on these grounds is the Scottish case of *John Saunders v. Scottish National Camps Association Ltd.*

Saunders had been employed as a maintenance worker at a camp for teenaged schoolchildren for two years when his employers learned that he was gay. They dismissed him, so he applied to an industrial tribunal which upheld the dismissal on the grounds 'that he was required to work daily with children of ages 10 to 18; that the employers considered that to be a risk to the children; that there is a body of opinion which takes that view; and that the probable views of many parents was a legitimate matter to take into consideration' (Betten 1993: 342). Two appeals failed. Saunders was not dismissed for anything he had done or on account of any demonstrated risk.

Do such cases indicate that homosexuals should be added to the list of protected classes? It is of interest to note that a review of the position of lesbians and gay men in the European Union legal order concludes that another strategy may be better. There are drawbacks if lesbians and gay men present themselves as victims or claim what others see as legal privileges. Any concentration on differences rather than similarities may reinforce prejudices. Human rights law embodies various positive concepts, such as equality, dignity, privacy, and free development or fulfilment of an individual's personality. The less favourable treatment of homosexuals can often be demonstrated to conflict with one of these (Clapham and Weiler 1993: 66–7). The argument can be illustrated by the case of *B v. France* brought before the European Court of Human Rights; it concerned not a homosexual but a transsexual, a male who had become female, and who wanted the reference to her sex in the registration of her birth to be brought up-to-date so that she could marry. The Court found in her favour, deciding that she

> finds herself daily in a situation which, taken as a whole, is not compatible with the respect due to her private life. Consequently, even having regard to the State's margin of appreciation, the fair balance which has to be struck between the general interest and the interests of the individual [. . .] has not been attained and there has thus been a violation of Article 8.
>
> (quoted from Waaldijk and Clapham 1993: 305)

The decision in the case of B centred on the protection of her private life and had no direct implications for the protection of other people. That issue has been raised when the age of consent for homosexual relations between men differs from either that for heterosexual relations or for homosexual relations between women. The European Commission of Human Rights (a body which assesses cases in order to decide which should be referred to the European Court of Human Rights) accepted arguments that male homosexuality is more frequent than female; that male homosexuals prefer young partners; that they frequently change partners; and that therefore young men are more exposed to the risks arising from homosexual relations than are young women. It concluded that 'while recognizing the changing and developing views on the issue' the difference in treatment (concerning the age of consent for gays compared with lesbians) satisfied the test of proportionality. The European Parliament, however, has urged Member States to apply to homosexuals the same age of consent as for heterosexual acts, and that has indeed been the recent trend (Waaldijk and Clapham 1993: 50, 196). Where the age of consent is different, it is often said that homosexuals are subjected to criminal conviction for activities which would have been lawful for heterosexuals, and that this is discriminatory. The argument assumes that anal and vaginal sexual intercourse are basically the same, which is a statement of personal belief and not of fact. If the assumption is rejected, then it is not discriminatory to treat the two kinds of sexual activity differently.

Positive principles can be utilized to combat discrimination most effectively in employment because there it is relatively easy to decide what things, people or skills are alike. For example, an organization can declare that all employees will be appointed and promoted in accordance with their individual abilities and performance. It can acknowledge that some posts require special qualifications, either as to individual skills or in order to avoid conflicts of interest and to protect the rights of other persons. An obvious example of the need to avoid public suspicions on this account, is that a police officer who in leisure time associates with known criminals is likely to disqualify himself or herself from employment in the police.

Whether sexual orientation is to be regarded as a private matter is a subject on which opinions differ sharply, often in association with religious belief. In few countries do people accept the clear separation of religion and state that is enforced in the USA. Many insist that their government should use all its powers to advance the cause of what they believe to be the true religion. Some consider homosexual practices contrary to their faith.

There can also be conflicts between individual desires and beliefs about the policies needed to promote collective interests. It can be held that the state has a duty to provide for the birth of a new generation sufficient in number and other qualities to replace the previous generation and assume the burden of supporting the elderly. The state has a further interest in the stability of the households in which children grow up; it is a burden upon the social services when there is an increase in the proportion of single-parent households. A government may feel obligated to manage its financial and other policies so as to support the kinds of family living it believes best. It can therefore legitimately offer incentives to bisexuals to lead a heterosexual existence while seeking to ensure equal treatment for homosexuals. If in pursuit of this latter policy it creates a protected class – as the Netherlands is doing – the scope of the protections needs as careful specification as those for linguistic minorities.

Family life raises more difficult issues regarding discrimination than does employment or the provision of services. For example, in Britain, applications from homosexual couples to adopt children will not normally succeed since it is believed to be in the interests of a child to grow up with two parents of opposite sex. Sometimes homosexual couples go through a form of marriage. Should such ceremonies be validated by churches? Should they be acknowledged and registered by the state? Should they create the same legal obligations as conventional marriage or should the partners draw up a private contract under civil law instead? Is a failure to recognize such unions discriminatory? Answers must depend upon views about whether a union between a couple of the same sex can be basically the same as one between a couple of opposite sex. Insofar as such unions frequently lead to the birth of children and to long-term responsibilities for their care, some will maintain that there is necessarily a fundamental difference; but some heterosexual unions are neither fertile nor intended to be, and many are of relatively short duration, so the problem of comparison is more difficult.

The legal position in Europe is the more complicated because some states have gone further than others in recognizing homosexual partnerships. A Danish law of 1989 makes it possible for a same-sex couple to enter into a 'registered partnership' at the town hall offices (but not in a church). Within Denmark this has most of the legal effects of marriage (especially in the fields of maintenance, property, inheritance, immigration, tax and social security). There have been some similar moves in the Netherlands and France. What then happens if a homosexual couple from Denmark move to another EU country? The European Commission on Human Rights has held that Member States may legitimately act to protect family life, but that homosexual relationships fall within the field of private life, not that of family life. The European Court of Justice has held that where a state allows rights to same sex couples of its own nationality it must allow a similar right to those of another EC nationality (Waaldijk and Clapham 1993: 40, 96–7, 197–8).

The question of whether parties to a same-sex relationship should have the same rights as parties to a marriage also arises on the death of a partner. In several EU countries the tax to be paid on inheritance (death duties) is higher in respect of a bequest to an unmarried lover. A surviving lesbian or gay partner may also find it difficult to obtain rights of succession to rented accommodation, even though he or she may have been living in the dwelling prior to the partner's death (Waaldijk 1993: 98–100).

These examples show that it can be hard to get agreement about an appropriate comparator. They suggest that the definitions of protected classes of persons and protected fields of activity must be carefully interrelated, and that it is frequently necessary to make exceptions to general rules. Any differences in treatment must, if they are to comply with European law, have objective justifications proportionate to the end to be achieved. The justifications should be explicit. To protect the rights of children or other people it may be necessary to restrict the rights of men and women, but all restrictions must be cogent and able to withstand reasoned challenge. Even so, there are problems with no obvious solutions. Many of those ready to defend Salman Rushdie's right to freedom of expression also accepted that there was a duty on the part of an author not wantonly to offend the deeply-felt sentiments of others. Societies differ greatly in their views about the offensiveness of the public display of sexuality of either a heterosexual or a homosexual character.

In the same week during July 1993 two reports pointed to continuing controversy about equality of treatment for homosexuals. In one, US President Clinton announced that a recruit to the armed services would no longer be asked about his or her sexual orientation, but that a self-declared homosexual or a person engaging in homosexual acts would still be subject to dismissal. The policy was summarized as 'don't ask, don't tell, don't pursue'. The policy will bear upon anyone engaging in homosexual behaviour irrespective of whether they have a homosexual identity. At the same time British Prime Minister Major indicated his support for lowering the age of consent to homosexual sex from 21 to 18. Many gay men would see such a change as only reducing the extent of the discrimination. Why should it not be 16? They testify that they had developed by that age as fixed a sexual identity as that developed by heterosexuals. Yet they would not be the only people to be affected by a change in the age of consent. The number of men who are not unambiguously either 'straight' or 'gay' is significant, and less seems to be known about the factors which influence their conduct. The controversies will continue, but it should be remembered that while the argument for 'gay rights' can be strengthened by a demonstration of discrimination, it does not depend upon this. Whether or not a difference is discriminatory is a technical question and not a moral one.

Laws regulating marriage and divorce, and providing remedies for the victims of discrimination, are the responsibility of governments. The international conventions set standards to which governments should conform when they legislate and also prohibit discrimination by governments. In the Netherlands it would be possible for someone to start proceedings in the constitutional court alleging that an act passed by the legislature contravened the principle of equal treatment enshrined in the constitution. Similar action is possible in the United States and many other countries, but not in Britain because of the doctrine of the supremacy of parliament. Parliament can do whatever it wants, and if it discriminates, its action cannot be invalidated, though the government has usually amended any legislation found to be in breach of international law. British citizens of Asian origin expelled from East African countries in the late 1960s and denied entrance to Britain found that they had a remedy against governmental discrimination under the European Convention on Human Rights. The Commission held that for them to be denied entry when others of a different race could exercise that right amounted to 'degrading treatment' within the meaning of Article 3 of the Convention. British immigration law has since been altered, but it is still accused of being racially discriminatory.

The European Convention on Human Rights was sponsored by the Council of Europe, an organization which includes as members Turkey and a number of East European states that are not (yet) members of the smaller group of states which forms the European

Union.The EU has its own court (the European Court of Justice) to adjudicate questions of its own law, and that sometimes has to take up questions of alleged discrimination, such as when it has had to rule upon the rights of a spouse. Until 1992 it was the position that the Indian husband of a French national was entitled to be admitted to the UK with his wife, but the Indian husband of a British woman had to meet the requirements of British immigration law. Mr Surinder Singh, an Indian national had, together with his British wife, been living and working in Germany. They then moved to Britain where he was held liable to deportation. The Court ruled in 1992 that the UK must allow Mr Singh rights under EU law; otherwise British citizens might be inhibited from exercising their right to free movement from the fear that their spouses might not be able to accompany them upon their return to the UK.

Conclusion

In fulfilment of international obligations and in response to the expectations of their own citizens, many states have legislated in order to promote equality of treatment within their own borders. International standards as to equality of treatment are being progressively recognized, though major differences remain. Some states have acceded to few human rights treaties; others have entered reservations when acceding. Within the EU the principles of subsidiarity and the 'margin of appreciation' permit a certain variation from one state to another.

The cases discussed in this chapter teach at least two important lessons: that a decision as to whether something is discriminatory depends upon the identification of an appropriate comparator; and that the selection of comparators raises different problems when seeking to ensure equal treatment for the various classes of persons to be protected. They also show the advisability of defining discrimination objectively and separating the decision of whether something is discriminatory from the decision of whether or not it is legally or morally right. The courts have to decide whether, in particular circumstances, it is lawful for an employer to terminate a woman's contract because she has become pregnant. Discrimination law has been stretched to enable them to do so, even though there is no masculine equivalent of pregnancy. The rights of parties to same-sex relationships can also be protected by stretching the definition of discrimination, but the protection need not be based upon an argument that it is discriminatory to treat them differently from opposite-sex relationships. Someone could maintain *both* that it is not discriminatory for a party to a same-sex relationship to be liable for higher death duties on an inheritance *and* that the level of duty should be the same in the two cases. The first statement turns upon whether the two kinds of relationship are thought to be basically the same, which is a belief about matters of fact. The second statement is a value judgement about what ought to be the case. The analysis of discrimination may help clarify moral problems but it cannot resolve them.

Postscript

The European Court of Justice has held that the EC directive on equal treatment 'recognised the legitimacy, in terms of the principle of equal treatment, first, of protecting a woman's biological condition during and after pregnancy, and second, of protecting the special relationship between a woman and her child over the period which followed pregnancy and childbirth.' It declared that there could be no question of comparing the situation of a pregnant woman with that of a man incapable of work for medical reasons because the Court had earlier drawn a clear distinction between pregnancy and illness. The woman dismissed because of pregnancy had suffered direct discrimination on the grounds of her sex (*Webb v EMO Air Cargo (UK) Ltd*). If the EC directive is of wider scope because it incorporates a protective principle, the Court's decision is not incompatible with the definition of discrimination as less favourable treatment used in this book.

An Australian court has also considered whether it is unlawful to exclude women from jobs entailing exposure to lead poisoning. In *Mount Isa Mines v Marks* the judge concluded that this was not discrimination on grounds of pregnancy, though it could be discrimination on grounds of health. He found that 'a woman who was seeking to become pregnant or a woman who was pregnant or a woman who was breast-feeding a child was not, in the lead industry, in the same or similar circumstances to a man, so their circumstances could not be compared.'

7

Conclusion

The twentieth century has seen the spread of the ideal of democracy from the political sphere to most fields of social life. The belief that humans are equal in dignity and rights has been strengthened by the institutions of mass society, particularly by an entertainment industry which develops the ordinary person's capacity to put himself or herself into the positions of others and to see life as they might see it. The development of empathy is crucial both to the recognition of discrimination and to attempts to reduce it. Within this movement of feeling the idea of discrimination has, since the late 1950s, come into increasing use to denote some act or practice which denies equality of treatment and is therefore objectionable. Those denied equal treatment often feel a more intense sense of grievance than is ever appreciated by people who escape such experiences. So in all probability appeals for help to eliminate discrimination will continue for several decades to evoke emotional reactions of either sympathy or exasperation.

Discrimination is both an idea that features in ordinary conversation and a concept in the social sciences. Economics, psychology and sociology all have something to say about its nature and causes, political science about institutions developed to combat it and human geography about the distribution of inequalities that may be associated with it. In considering why discrimination persists, it can be useful to recall the concept of a colour tax explained at page 13, and to relate it to the account at pages 29–30 of the estate agent who pretended to check with landlords about the availability of accommodation. Discrimination always has a price, but often this is not apparent. When landlords are faced with the alternatives of letting accommodation or leaving it vacant, many will reach a decision in line with their financial interests. Many will take the minority applicant who can be charged a little more. But often the discriminator is not faced with so clear a choice. In this instance it was the estate agent who was taking the decisons. The landlord never learned about the would-be tenants from the minority ethnic groups. There was, of course, a cost to the estate agency, which was turning away business, but if demand was high relative to supply, the cost may not have been great and probably had no impact upon the pay received at the end of the week by the person who was making the telephone calls.

Legislators have built upon the understanding provided by social science to provide both international and national protections and remedies. Yet examination of what is entailed also raises philosophical issues. Chapter 6 has sought to clarify the moral principle underlying the concept: like things should be treated alike; unlike things should be treated in accordance with their differences. Sometimes discrimination is defined as differential treatment occasioned by irrelevant unlikenesses, but it should by now be clear that it can be very difficult to decide what is legally and morally irrelevant in particular cases. Public opinion in these matters can change, and, for example, is now much more tolerant than 40 years ago of claims to equality of treatment irrespective of gender, race and sexual orientation. The discussion of some of the more problematic examples, such as some of those affecting homosexuals, and consideration of policies to combat disadvantage, should have reinforced the thesis advanced in the Introduction: that it is best to define discrimination objectively, as differential treatment, and to consider separately whether it is unlawful or immoral. It should also have demonstrated the value of discussing lawful discrimination. Employers should not discriminate, but a film director selecting an actor to play the part of Martin Luther King or Malcolm X should be able to limit the search to black men. An employer seeking to correct a racial imbalance in the work force should be able to take certain forms of 'positive action'.

Any form of selection is a kind of discrimination, but the word becomes more useful when an adjective is attached to it specifying the ground of discrimination, e.g., gender, race, religion, etc. To talk of discrimination in general is not empty of meaning, because it makes it possible to compare the different grounds and the characteristics of the different protected classes to which they give rise. Whether this can be an illuminating exercise the reader can now decide for himself or herself. The comparison shows that while laws against discrimination necessarily create protected classes they also create new problems. This is particularly important when the laws prohibit not only conscious or direct discrimination ('differential treatment' in the USA) but also unconscious discrimination or indirect discrimination ('unjustified differential impact' in the USA). In the second (but not the first) case an aggrieved person has first to establish that he or she is a member of a protected class in order to be able to claim a remedy; this is not always easy and the very procedure can be criticized because it treats the protected class as an objective reality when (as most obviously in the case of race) it is only a product of bias on the part of the discriminators.

The book has also tried to bring out how important it is for the law to define the protected field and for the courts to be clear about who is to be compared to whom. Discrimination can be unlawful only in specified relationships: to determine whether a woman has been treated less favourably than a man would have been, it is necessary to consider what would have happened to a comparable man in comparable circumstances. When it comes to pregnancy, this, too, is difficult. Sometimes it is necessary to make exceptions to the protected field in order to protect the rights or interests of other people. Chapter 6 suggested that decisions about the relative rights to equal treatment of the parties to a sexual union may in future be influenced more directly by the legal recognition of the rights of the child.

The movement to promote greater equality of treatment will have to continue for some decades to rely upon the concepts of discrimination and of protected classes, but the first signs have appeared of an alternative approach which may well supercede them. This is the attempt to develop, from the Universal Declaration of Human Rights and from regional human rights instruments, positive conceptions of the rights of all humans, particularly rights to respect for their dignity as individuals, their ways of life and their personal development. At present these concepts often have only a rhetorical value as abstract ideals, but human rights law has started to give them content. International tribunals use them as criteria to influence the actions of governments. As R.J. Vincent (1986: 93) noted, this is revolutionary! By accepting an obligation under the United Nations Charter to promote respect for human rights and fundamental freedoms, governments did two new things. They added the needs and interests of individuals and groups other than states to their traditional preoccupation with peace and security among themselves. By taking on these purposes they dissolved international society into a world society in which groups and individuals can have equal standing with states. This revolution has succeeded only in those countries which are prepared voluntarily to accept the jurisdiction of international tribunals. Elsewhere it is far from complete, as has been demonstrated by the failure of world society to prevent flagrant forms of discrimination in the former Yugoslavia and in many other countries where there is no trust between groups. The only feasible response to such tragedies is to continue with the struggle to reinforce and extend international law.

Further Reading

1 Introduction

An excellent and simple introduction to the international law of human rights is to be found in Sieghart (1986).

References to United Nations publications require frequent updating, so it can be useful to seek advice from the United Nations Information Centres located in various major cities. The London Centre is at 20 Buckingham Gate, SW1E 6LB. Other centres are at:

- 40 avenue de Broqueville, 1200 Brussels, Belgium.
- 37 H.C. Andersen Boulevard, DK 1553 Copenhagen, Denmark.
- Rua Latino Coelho no 1, Edificio Aviz, Bloco A1-10, 1000 Lisbon, Portugal.
- PO Box 3400, 28020 Madrid, Spain.
- PO Box 1068, Lagos, Nigeria.
- 1 rue Miollis, 75732 Paris Cedex 15, France.
- Palazzetto Venezia, Piazzo San Marco 50, Rome, Italy.
- PO Box 4045, Sydney, NSW 2001, Australia.
- Shin Aoyama Building Nishika floor 22, 1-1 Minami Aoyama 1-chome, Minato-ku, Tokyo 107, Japan.
- PO Box 500, A-1400 Vienna, Austria.
- 1889 F Street, NW, Washington, DC, USA.

A major reference work is *United Nations Action in the Field of Human Rights* (1993 edition). The texts of conventions can be found in *A Compilation of International Instruments*, while information about which states have acceded to them, and any reservations they have entered, is in a companion volume entitled *Status of International Instruments*. Most readers would find the information they seek best set out in a series of popular booklets, called *Human Rights Fact Sheets*, each of which takes up a particular topic. They can also be obtained by writing to the UN Human Rights Centre, Palais des Nations, CH 1211 Geneva 10. In addition the UN publishes the *Bulletin of Human Rights* which contains articles for a general readership but written by specialists. The International Labour Office is at CH 1211 Geneva 22.

An introductory account of thought concerning racial differences may be found in Banton (1988). For a complementary discussion, see Rex (1986). For information on the kinds of legal problems which can be presented by differences of custom between ethnic groups, Poulter (1986) is particularly helpful. Some may find it too detailed but the problems in question cannot be regulated without close attention to detail.

2 Supply and Demand

On differences in labour supply, consult Chiswick (1979) and (1988). Readers who have studied economics should appreciate the analysis of discrimination in Lundahl and Wadensjö (1984). Dex (1986) and Phelps (1972) are also recommended.

Analysis of economic structure has to grapple with fairly complex statistical sources, as can be seen from Owen and Green (1992).

3 Locating Discrimination

For the report on medical school admissions, see CRE (1988).

For an economist's study of discrimination in housing, based on the purchase of houses by Asians in suburban Manchester, see Fenton (1976), while the experimental study is described in CRE (1990). The thorough examination of the allocation of dwellings in Hackney is set out in CRE (1984). Smith (1977) is strongly recommended and MacEwen (1991) useful.

For summaries of the findings from situation testing in Australia, Canada, France, the Netherlands, United Kingdom, and the United States, see Bovenkerk (1992). This is a manual describing procedures which are to be followed in an 11-country comparative study of racial discrimination being conducted by the International Labour Office.

The annual report of the CRE (10-12 Allington Street, London SW1E 5EH) contains much information on individual cases and upon investigations. The annual report of the (British) Equal Opportunities Commission (published by Her Majesty's Stationery Office) is more general.

The quarterly *Journal of Ethnic and Migration Studies* (formerly *New Community*) contains up-to-date articles relating to Britain and West European countries. They are written by specialists but in a style that makes research findings accessible to the general reader.

4 Protections from Discrimination

For information and reading on international instruments, see the references to the UN under reading for Chapter 1. Developments in this area are subject to continuous change. For current developments see the *Human Rights Monitor* published by the International Service for Human Rights, PO Box 16, CH 1211 Geneva 20 cic. The work of the human rights treaty bodies is helped by a variety of non-governmental organizations such as Amnesty International, 1 Easton Street, London WC1X 8DJ and the Minority Rights Group, 379 Brixton Road, London SW9 7DE. A similar organization with a special concern for the racial convention is ARIS (Anti-Racism Information Service), 14 Avenue Trembley, 1209 Geneva, Switzerland. Jacobson (1992) offers a rather formal introduction to the work of CEDAW.

The case for a new law to protect the rights of disabled people in Britain is set out in Bynoe *et al*. (1991).

5   Remedies and their Effectiveness

As yet there have been few attempts to compare the effectivess of different remedies, but the outcomes of individual cases can be seen in some of the references for Chapter 4. Palmer (1992) is a handbook for legal practitioners but it sets out the provisions of British law simply and clearly and can be recommended to any reader with an interest in the laws against sex and race discrimination. Collins (1992) expresses personal value judgements, but it has a chapter on AIDS and HIV and chapters on all the EC countries. For a comprehensive survey of Lesbian and Gay Rights in European Law and Policy coordinated by the European Human Rights Foundation, see Waaldijk and Clapham (1993), obtainable in the UK from Stonewall, 2 Greycoat Place, London SW1P 1SB.

An excellent discussion of the moral issues raised by quota policies is provided in Edwards (1987).

6   Equal Treatment

The Johnson Controls case is discussed in an essay in Quest (1992) by Ellen Frankel Paul, 'Fetal protection, women's rights, and freedom of contract'. This argues against the equalization of opportunities by placing financial burdens upon employers. The volume of essays in which it appears draws mainly upon experience in the United States and is a useful corrective to some writing on this topic, but it tends to oppose the categories male and female and to neglect both the differences within these categories and the continuities between them.

References

Banton, Michael (1988) *Racial Consciousness*. London: Longman.

Banton, Michael (1990) Racial discrimination at work: Bristol cases. *New Community*, 17: 134–9.

Betten, Lammy (1993) Rights in the workplace, in Waaldijk, Kees and Clapham, Andrew, *Homosexuality: A European Community Issue*. International Studies in Human Rights Vol. 26. Dordrecht: Nijhoff, pp. 335–59.

Bovenkerk, Frank (1992) *Testing Discrimination in Natural Experiments. A Manual for International Comparative Research on Discrimination on the Grounds of 'Race' and Ethnic Origin*. Geneva: International Labour Office.

Brown, Colin and Gay, Pat (1985) *Racial Discrimination: 17 Years after the Act*. London: Policy Studies Institute Report 646.

Bynoe, Ian, Oliver, Mike and Barnes, Colin (1991) *Equal Rights for Disabled People*. London: Institute for Public Policy Research.

Chiswick, Barry R. (1979) The economic progress of immigrants: some apparently universal patterns, in Fellner, William (ed.) *Contemporary Economic Problems 1979*. Washington: American Enterprise Institute, pp. 357–99.

Chiswick, Barry R. (1988) Differences in education and earnings across racial and ethnic groups: tastes, discrimination, and investments in child quality. *The Quarterly Journal of Economics*, 103: 571–97.

Clapham, Andrew, and Weiler, J.H.H. (1993) Lesbians and gay men in the European Community legal order, in Waaldijk, Kees, and Clapham, Andrew, *Homosexuality: A European Community Issue*. International Studies in Human Rights Vol. 26. Dordrecht: Nijhoff, pp. 1–69.

Collins, Helen (1992) *The Equal Opportunities Handbook: A Guide to Law and Best Practice in Europe*. Oxford: Blackwell.

Colliver, Sandra (ed.) (1992) *Striking a Balance: Hate Speech, Freedom of Expression and Non-discrimination*. London: Article 19.

Commission for Racial Equality (1984) *Race and Council Housing in Hackney*. London: CRE.

Commission for Racial Equality (1988) *Medical School Admissions*. London: CRE.

Commission for Racial Equality (1990) *Sorry, It's Gone: Testing for Racial Discrimination in the Private Sector*. London: CRE.

Coussey, Mary (1992) The effectiveness of strategic enforcement of the Race Relations Act 1976, in Hepple, Bob and Szyszczak, Erika M. (eds) *Discrimination: The Limits of the Law*. London: Mansell, pp. 35–49.

Dex, Shirley (1986) *The Costs of Discriminating: A Review of the Literature*. Research and Planning Unit Paper 39. London: Home Office.

Dikötter, Frank (1992) *The Discourse of Race in Modern China*. London: Hurst.

Edwards, John (1987) *Positive Discrimination, Social Justice, and Social Policy*. London: Tavistock.

Fenton, Mike (1976) Price discrimination under non-monopolistic conditions. *Applied Economics*, 8: 135–44.

Hood, Roger (1992) *Race and Sentencing*. Oxford: Clarendon Press.

Home Office (1988) *Criminal Statistics, England and Wales, 1987*. London: HMSO.

Home Office (1989) *The 1988 British Crime Survey*. Home Office Research Study 111. London: HMSO.

Home Office (1991a) *Prison Statistics, England and Wales, 1990*. London: HMSO.

Home Office (1991b) *A Digest of Information on the Criminal Justice System*. London: Home Office Research and Statistics Department.

Ineichen, Bernard (1981) The housing decisions of young people. *British Journal of Sociology*, 32: 252–8.

Jacobson, Roberta (1992) The Committee on the Elimination of Discrimination Against Women, in Alston, Philip (ed.) *The United Nations and Human Rights: A Critical Appraisal*. Oxford: Clarendon Press, pp. 444–72.

Jowell, Roger and Airey, Colin (eds) (1991) *British Social Attitudes*, Eighth Report. Aldershot: Gower.

Lundahl, Mats, and Wadensjö, Eskil (1984) *Unequal Treatment: A Study in the Neo-Classical Theory of Discrimination*. New York University Press and London: Croom Helm.

MacEwen, Martin (1991) *Housing, Race and Law: The British Experience*. London: Routledge.

McCrudden, Christopher, Smith, David J. and Brown, Colin (1991) *Racial Justice at Work*. London: Policy Studies Institute.

MacIver, Robert M. (1948) *The More Perfect Union*. New York: Macmillan.

Owen, David, and Green, Anne (1992) Labour market experience and change among ethnic groups in Britain. *New Community*, 19: 1–6.

Palmer, Camilla (1992) *Discrimination at Work: The Law on Sex and Race Discrimination*, 2nd edn. London: Legal Action Group.

Phelps, Edmund S. (1972) The statistical theory of racism and sexism. *American Economic Review*, 62: 659–61.

Poulter, Sebastian M. (1986) *English Law and Ethnic Minority Customs*. London: Butterworths.

Quest, Caroline (ed.) (1992) *Equal Opportunities: A Feminist Fallacy*. London: Institute of Economic Affairs Health and Welfare Unit.

Rex, John (1986) *Race and Ethnicity*. Milton Keynes: Open University Press.

Rose, E.J.B. *et al.* (1969) *Colour and Citizenship: A Report on British Race Relations*. London: Oxford University Press.

Sieghart, Paul (1986) *The Lawful Rights of Mankind*. Oxford: Oxford University Press.

Smith, David J. (1977) *Racial Disadvantage in Britain: The PEP Report*. Harmondsworth: Penguin.

Townshend-Smith, Richard (1989) *Sex Discrimination in Employment: Law, Practice and Theory*. 2nd edn. London: Sweet & Maxwell.

Vincent, R.J. (1986) *Human Rights and International Relations*. Cambridge: Cambridge University Press.

Waaldijk, Kees (1993) The legal situation in the member states, in Waaldijk, Kees, and Clapham, Andrew, *Homosexuality: A European Community Issue*. International Studies in Human Rights Vol. 26. Dordrecht: Nijhoff, pp. 71–103.

Waaldijk, Kees and Clapham, Andrew (1993) *Homosexuality: A European Community Issue*. International Studies in Human Rights Vol. 26. Dordrecht: Nijhoff.

Walker, Monica A. (1989) The court disposal and remands of white, Afro-Caribbean and Asian men (London, 1983). *British Journal of Criminology*, 29: 353–67.

Yinger, John M., Galster, George, Smith, Barton and Eggers, Fred (1979) *The Status of Research into Racial Discrimination and Segregation in American Housing Markets: A Research Agenda for the Department of Housing and Urban Development*. Occasional Papers in Housing and Community Affairs, Vol. 6.

Index

RACE AND ETHNICITY

John Rex

Race and ethnicity, though key topics in the political sociology of the modern world, have remained problematic as concepts through the complexity of their interrelation with social structure. In this book, John Rex clarifies these problems and indicates the nature of the relationship between race and ethnicity on the one hand and the class and status order on the other, in both colonial and metropolitan societies. While the emphasis of the book is on the conceptual understanding of race and ethnicity, this is also related to historical and contemporary issues in race relations, such as those of institutional racism and multi-culturalism.

Contents

Sociological concepts and the field of ethnic and race relations – Race and ethnicity in sociological theory – Race, ethnicity and the structure of colonial society – Class, race and ethnicity in the metropolis – Benign and malign ethnicity – Racism, institutionalized and otherwise – The concept of a multi-cultural society – Bibliography – Index.

160pp   0 335 15385 2 (Paperback)   0 335 15386 0 (Hardback)